£15·00

The Risk Ranking Technique

in

Decision Making

Pergamon Titles of Related Interest

CHICKEN
Risk Assessment for Hazardous Installations

FULLWOOD & HALL
Probabilistic Risk Assessment in the Nuclear Power Industry

MOULD
Chernobyl: The Real Story

MURRAY
Nuclear Energy, 3rd Edition

PERSHAGEN
Light Water Reactor Safety

Pergamon Related Journals *(free specimen copy gladly sent on request)*

Building and Environment

Computers and Structures

Forensic Engineering

International Journal of Engineering Science

International Journal of Rock Mechanics and Mining Sciences

Journal of Terramechanics

Tunnelling and Underground Space Technology

The Risk Ranking Technique

in

Decision Making

JOHN C. CHICKEN

J. C. Consultancy Ltd, Godalming, Surrey, UK, and
John C. Chicken Consultancy GmbH, Langenargen, FRG

and

MICHAEL R. HAYNS

United Kingdom Atomic Energy Authority,
Harwell Laboratory, Didcot, Oxon, UK

PERGAMON PRESS
OXFORD · NEW YORK · BEIJING · FRANKFURT
SÃO PAULO · SYDNEY · TOKYO · TORONTO

U.K.	Pergamon Press plc, Headington Hill Hall, Oxford OX3 0BW, England
U.S.A.	Pergamon Press, Inc., Maxwell House, Fairview Park, Elmsford, New York 10523, U.S.A.
PEOPLE'S REPUBLIC OF CHINA	Pergamon Press, Room 4037, Qianmen Hotel, Beijing, People's Republic of China
FEDERAL REPUBLIC OF GERMANY	Pergamon Press GmbH, Hammerweg 6, D-6242 Kronberg, Federal Republic of Germany
BRAZIL	Pergamon Editora Ltda, Rua Eça de Queiros, 346, CEP 04011, Paraiso, São Paulo, Brazil
AUSTRALIA	Pergamon Press Australia Pty Ltd., P.O. Box 544, Potts Point, N.S.W. 2011, Australia
JAPAN	Pergamon Press, 5th Floor, Matsuoka Central Building, 1-7-1 Nishishinjuku, Shinjuku-ku, Tokyo 160, Japan
CANADA	Pergamon Press Canada Ltd., Suite No. 271, 253 College Street, Toronto, Ontario, Canada M5T 1R5

Copyright © 1989 J. C. Chicken and M. R. Hayns

First edition 1989

Library of Congress Cataloging in Publication Data
Chicken, John C.
The risk ranking technique in decision making/
John C. Chicken and Michael R. Hayns.—1st ed.
p.   cm.
Bibliography: p.
Includes index.
1. Decision-making.   2. Risk assessment.
I. Hayns, Michael R.   II. Title.
T57.95.C47   1989   658.4'03—dc19   89–31105

British Library Cataloguing in Publication Data
Chicken, John C. (John Charles) *1926–*
The risk ranking technique in decision making.
1. Risk management
I. Title   II. Hayns, Michael R.
658.4'03
ISBN 0–08–037212–0

In order to make this volume available as economically and as rapidly as possible the author's typescript has been reproduced in its original form. This method unfortunately has its typographical limitations but it is hoped that they in no way distract the reader.

Printed in Great Britain by BPCC Wheatons Ltd, Exeter

Contents

Contents

Preface

There have been many excellent proposals for aids to decision making. Most of these proposals tend to deal with only one group of the factors that have to be considered in assessing the acceptability of major high technology projects. In this book we develop a comprehensive approach, known as the Ranking Technique, for the assessment of decision options. The aim being to provide a way of presenting a decision maker with a consistent way of making a comprehensive assessment of all the factors associated with complex decisions. The Ranking Technique we describe, while being based on a thorough and detailed analysis of all the issues involved, presents the results of the analysis in a simple transparent and justifiable way that should be understandable by the lay public not versed in the complexities of the issues involved. In our presentation of the Ranking Technique we attempt to justify the logical basis of the Technique and to describe how it can be applied. Although we illustrate the use of the Ranking Technique by post hoc application to only four major decisions that caused controversy and one fuel resource evaluation we stress the Technique is applicable to all decision making situations. It is our contention that the Technique provides a logical and justifiable approach to the assessment of decision options, which should be useful both to those directly involved in the decision making process and to students of decision making.

The study describes how technical, economic and socio-political factors can be evaluated and their significance integrated to give a comprehensive assessment of the decision options. Appendices to the study describe: the essential features of the Ranking Technique, definition of the terms used in the study, a review of some technical acceptability criteria that have been used and an outline of the essential steps in reactor licensing procedure.

We hope all that read this study will find that it shows ways in which the decision making processes they are associated with can be improved in a rational and logical way.

JCC
MRH

List of Figures

List of Tables

List of Tables

TABLES IN APPENDICES

Chapter 1
Introduction

Quotations from "The Official Rules",*
Ashley-Perry's fifth statistical axiom:
"The product of an arithmetical computation
is the answer to an equation: it is not the
solution to a problem."
Thurber's conclusion: "There is no safety in
numbers, or in anything else."

Starting from the challenge of the two quotations above this study
examines how in reality complex decisions can be made more effectively
with the assistance of objective and logical disciplines. The type of
decision particularly considered is a final decision about whether or
not a project goes ahead. It is assumed the decision maker involved
will have overall responsibility for making the decision in a clearly
defensible way on the best information available. It is not assumed
that the decision maker is an expert in every field involved but it is
assumed that he has access to any additional expert opinion that may
be required. More specifically the aim of the study is to critically
examine the capability of the Risk Ranking Technique for dealing
effectively with a variety of complex decision making situations,
including decisions related to controversial projects and projects
that involve assessing the acceptability of major risks, when every
associated factor from technical characteristics to public opinion has
to be taken into account.   The incentive for developing the Risk
Ranking Technique was the need to provide decision makers with a
method for making comprehensive assessments in a way that deals
consistently with the matrix of factors involved. In developing the
technique the aim was to provide decision makers whether at the
political or industrial level with a transparent and defensible way of
arriving at decisions. Even for smaller decisions in which only a
single range of factors need be considered the technique provides a
logical structure to the assessment of the options involved. The
basis of the Ranking Technique is the comprehensive assessment of all
the associated technical, economic and socio-political factors. The
Technique, which is described at length in references 1 and 2 and is
summarized in Appendix 1, consists of assessing the acceptability of
each of the factors involved and scoring the results of the assessment
on a scale of 0-4. The higher the score the lower the acceptability,
the overall Ranking of acceptability being determined by integrating
the scores of the individual factors. The Ranking that an activity is
given will provide the decision maker, whether at the regulatory level
or the project management level with a yardstick to judge in a
consistent way how acceptable the activity is.

By the nature of the circumstances of decision making, decisions often
have to be made under conditions when the data about the subject of
the decision are sparse and uncertain. Such circumstances are not

---

*Paul Dickson's "Official Rules", published Arrow Books, London 1981.

1

unusual in decision making in business or in scientific and technological developments. Unless solutions are found to these problems developments that could be useful to society may be inhibited. To overcome these inherently complex problems several techniques have been proposed. Part of this study is devoted to evaluating the techniques currently available and comparing their efficacy with the Risk Ranking Technique.

Among the many general texts on decision making, Koutsoyiannis' "Non Price Decisions"[3] and Matthew Miles and Michael Huberman's "Qualitative Data Analysis" are particularly useful.[4] Very practical and direct guides to the subject are given by: Myra Chapman in her "Decision Analysis",[5] Maurice Preston's "Statistical Decision Theory"[6] and Gordon Hilton's "Intermediate Politometrics".[7] The methods they describe are of considerable help in arranging and evaluating complex evidence in a logical way that assists the decision maker to reach a verdict. David Pearce's "Decision Making for Energy Futures", which was based on a study of the Windscale Inquiry for the Social Science Research Council, shows clearly the complex range of factors that have to be considered in government policy decisions.[8]

Like any analytical techniques decision analysis techniques have their limits and should not be used uncritically. It is therefore vital that the suitability of a technique for assessing a particular problem is determined before any value is given to its results. Determination of the suitability of a method includes assessing whether or not relevant data exists and if data exists how exactly they fit the case being examined. In the evaluation of a new or novel process data that precisely fits the specific case is unlikely to be available and any evaluation has to be based on synthetic data. Synthesizing data is a process that by its very nature involves uncertainty. This does not mean a novel process will fail, it simply means it is not known with absolute certainty how successful it will be. The Space Programme illustrates how success can be achieved and the cost that may be involved when there is little relevant data.

The analyst, the techniques used and the stage in a project's life at which the assessment is made all influence the decision making. The changes in the relevance of the results of an assessment that take place with the passage of time can be quite dramatic. Unless the decision is made and implemented in the same instant the need for the decision may change and the relative significance of the associated factors may change.

Judging the efficacy of a decision making process is not simple. One method is to assess how acceptable the decisions proposed are to those affected by them, another method is to assess how successful past decisions made on the basis of a particular decision making process have been. Judging success has, like so many aspects of decision making, many qualitative aspects. But techniques exist to help the making of such judgements. Central to any judgement of the efficacy of decision making techniques is determination of the decision making environment. In this study the Ranking Technique is tested on five major proposals, which have given rise to a certain amount of public concern. These tests show how effective the Technique can be in predicting the most acceptable decision.

Although the capability of the Ranking Technique is demonstrated on five quite different proposals the examples do not define the limits of the Technique or the most likely users. The Technique is intended mainly for assessing complex decisions where the way account is taken of the whole matrix of technical, economic and socio-political factors has to be clear and defensible. Even though the Technique is designed to deal comprehensively with the whole matrix of factors involved in complex decisions it can be used when the decision is related to just one factor. The decision makers to whom the Technique is likely to be of most interest will be at either a senior political or a senior industrial level and with responsibility for justifying and defending project decisions in terms of the technical content, financial implications or socio-political acceptability.

In the following the analysis of the capability of Ranking Technique as an aid to complex decision making is built up in ten steps. The steps are:

1) The problems of decision making particularly when the decision involves the acceptability of major risks.
2) The relevance of decision analysis techniques currently available.
3) The nature of the Ranking Technique.
4) Evaluation of technical factors for Ranking.
5) Evaluation of economic factors for Ranking.
6) Evaluation of socio-political factors for Ranking.
7) Assessment of the efficacy of the Ranking Technique in five cases.
8) The basis for alternatives to the Ranking Technique in decision making.
9) Guidelines for the use of the Ranking Technique.
10) The overall conclusions suggested and future developments.

Some of the terms used in the study may, in general usage, have several meanings, so to prevent any misunderstanding the meaning attributed to them in this study are specified in Appendix 2.

Chapter 2
The Problems of Decision Making

Decision making takes many forms but the type of decisions that are the main concern of this study are those involving the evaluation of many complex factors, which are difficult to evaluate comprehensively in a uniform and consistent way. It is characteristic of such decisions that they have to be made in a transparently justifiable way and not on the basis of some capricious whim. The importance of transparency being that it allows it to be seen, by all interested parties, that all the relevant technical, economic and moral issues have been considered. Such decisions may arise in companies or at national or international government level. To clarify the types of decision making problems considered first the main types of decision are described and categorised, then the nature of the problems associated with each category of decision are assessed. From this assessment conclusions are drawn about the way the Ranking Technique is most likely to help each type of decision making situation.

Decision making can be described in deceptively simple terms, such as "agreeing the course of action required". Such simple definitions miss many of the important nuances associated with the various parts of the decision making process. For an examination of the various types of decision making process to lay any claim to being thorough it must identify not only the nature of the demands for a decision, the goal of a decision and the consequences of a decision, but also the environment the decision making process has to operate in. The whole environment is often conditioned by the fact that there is a need to be able to show how a particular decision was reached. This need may arise from: those directly involved in decision making, from the people affected by the decision, the general public and out of consideration for those following who must operate future decision making activities.

The first step towards identifying the various types of decision is to identify the essential elements of the environment that may surround any decision making process. In reference 9 a model of the environment of policy making was proposed and that model is used as the foundation for the model of the environment of the decision making process used in this study, as the processes are closely related. The decision making environment is seen as just one part of the universal environment set which includes all real and transcendental systems sets. Transcendental systems sets are those sets outside present knowledge, so only real systems sets are relevant to this discussion. Real system sets include: designed physical system sets, human activity system sets, designed abstract system sets and social and cultural systems sets. Designed physical system sets embrace all the inanimate products of man's activity such as machines and factories. Human activity systems are defined as all systems that exist as a result of human endeavour like cities, political systems and computer systems. Designed abstract system sets represent the knowledge man has developed. Social and cultural system sets in some way overlap

the human activity systems sets and the designed abstract systems
sets. The elements of the real systems set most relevant to the
decision making process are shown diagrammatically in a simplified
form in Figure 1. One variable the figure does not show is time. The
influence of time is ubiquitous it influences impartially both the
explained and the explanatory variables in the argument. Time has to
be allowed for in the assessment of each variable.

Each of the elements identified represents a complete group of
relevant factors so that taken together the elements define all the
factors that make up the environment surrounding the decision making
process. The significance of any factor may vary with time. For
example, in a major project the importance of financial resources is
different at the conceptual stage when the demand for funding is low
compared with the construction stage when the demand for funding is
real and can be very significant even in national terms. Table 1
summarizes the ways the environment surrounding a decision may change
with time. Attention is particularly drawn to the fact that with the
passage of time the need for a decision may either increase or
decrease.

TABLE 1   SUMMARY OF CHANGES POSSIBLE WITH TIME IN THE
DECISION MAKING ENVIRONMENT

DECISION VARIABLE	CHANGES THAT MAY OCCUR WITH THE PASSAGE OF TIME
KNOWLEDGE	Improved knowledge may show action no longer required or must be modified
RESOURCE REQUIREMENT	Demand for resources in terms of material, finance or manpower may be different to that originally predicted.
REQUIREMENT FOR DECISION	Demand for decision and action may increase or decrease

The need for a decision can, with some justification, be described as
being generated by various elements in the environment surrounding the
decision making process. For this study the decision making process is
defined as: the interaction between elements within the decision
making set that result in determination of how demands that arise can
be most acceptably satisfied with the resources available. This
concept of decision making being an interaction between the related
elements of a set is illustrated in Figure 2, which shows the decision
making process being a continuum lasting from the emergence of the
demand to the satisfaction of the demand. During the time of the
decision making process the significance of the various variables
involved may change. In a decision involving a scientific or
technological development the changes that have to be allowed for in
knowledge may be quite dramatic.

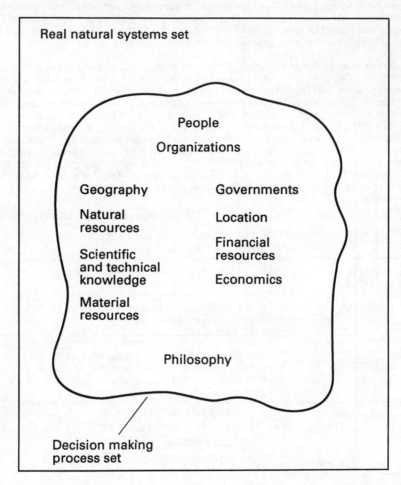

Fig 1 Elements of the real systems set relevant to the decision
       making process set

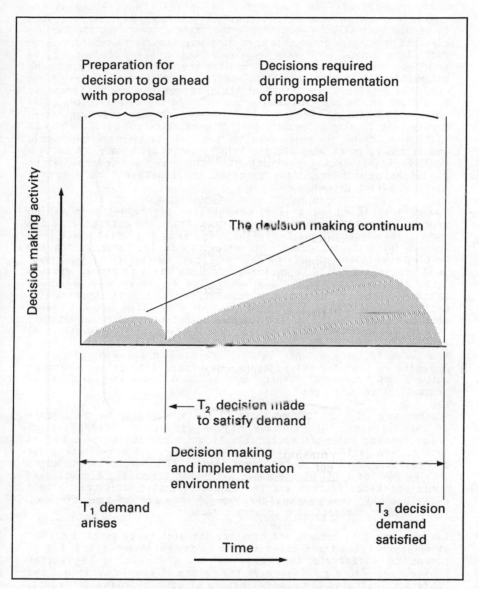

Fig 2 Decision making continuum

The dots in the diagrammatic representation of the continuum represent the interactions between the elements involved, the number of dots being proportional to the number of interactions. Although the continuum is shown two dimensionally it could perhaps be described three dimensionally to demonstrate the interactions with the various elements involved. Interactions in many ways amount to subordinate or partial decisions, with main decision processes being completed by T_2 and T_3. Generally there is a peak in the intensity of the interactions some time before the completion of the main modes in the decision process. The nature of the interactions are different at each stage in the decision making process. In the case illustrated it was assumed action necessary to implement the decision was taken. However, it is also recognized that in some cases the decision may be to take no action, in which case the decision making continuum would end at the T_2 point when the preliminary decision is made. Also in a real decision making environment there may be several major decisions, which are interdependent and together form a formal decision making procedure.

Having identified the general composition of the decision making process, attention is now given to identifying and categorizing the main types of decision. Decisions range from the small which only involve insignificant demands on resources, to the large, which may involve commitment of nationally significant quantities of resources. Small decisions could be deciding how many bolts to order, while a large decision could be deciding whether or not to order a new power station. Between these two extremes there is a whole spectrum of decision sizes. The size or importance of a decision does not give a complete description of a decision, the associated risk or uncertainty is also an important parameter that has to be evaluated in assessing the implications of the various decision options. In this context the terms "risk" and "uncertainty" are used in the way defined in Appendix 2, that is, "risk" means the probability of an undesired outcome and "uncertainty" that there is doubt about the quantitative or qualitative data used.

Another way decisions can be categorized is according to the purpose of the decision. The purpose may be domestic, internal to an organization, external nationally to an organization or external internationally to an organization, regulatory in the national sense or regulatory in the international sense. Complex decisions which involve consideration of the whole matrix of technical, economic and socio-political factors are termed comprehensive decisions. Simple decisions may involve consideration of only part of the matrix of factors such as technical or economic factors.

Tables 2 and 3 illustrate and classify the various types of decision. It is appreciated the classification is somewhat arbitrary, but it serves to illustrate the range of decision making situations considered. Table 2 illustrates the nature of simple decisions and Table 3 illustrates the general nature of comprehensive decisions. Examination of Tables 2 and 3 suggests that some simple decisions may not justify extensive use of decision making aids. The main requirement is that the decision maker involved has the necessary analytical training and skills. In that context an appreciation of the Ranking Technique logic will be useful in developing the right analytical approach. In addition to a decision maker being equipped with the right analytical approach, there is no escape from the requirement that a decision maker should have access to expert advice on every facet of the decisions to be dealt with.

TABLE 2 THE NATURE OF SIMPLE DECISIONS

SIZE OF DECISION
(Illustrative Examples)

SCOPE OF DECISION	SMALL	MEDIUM	LARGE
ORGANIZA-TIONAL	Deciding how to design a small component of secondary significance	Deciding which machine to buy	Deciding to extend production facilities
NATIONAL	Deciding to adopt a new technical standard	Deciding which design to adopt for a nationally marketed product	Deciding the level for a major nation-ally marketed commodity
INTER-NATIONAL	Deciding to adopt an international system of units	Deciding to join and participate in an interna-tional research project	Deciding that an organiza-tion should operate in several countries
REGULATORY	Deciding which factories to inspect	Deciding the level of contamination that must not be exceeded	Deciding a specific plant must be subject to detailed assessment before it can be allowed to operate

By definition comprehensive decisions involve, to some extent, consideration of the: technical, economic and socio-political groups of factors. It was to deal with such disparate factors that the Ranking Technique was devised. The adequacy of the Ranking Technique for providing an easily understood, clear and comprehensive evaluation of the evidence available and giving the decision maker a coherent, consistent and logical way of assessing of the merits of various options available is examined in the analysis that follows in later chapters.

TABLE 3   ILLUSTRATIONS OF THE GENERAL NATURE OF
COMPREHENSIVE DECISIONS

SCOPE OF DECISION	SIZE OF DECISION (Illustrative Examples)		
	SMALL	MEDIUM	LARGE
ORGANIZA-TIONAL	A decision by a committee to accept a research project	A decision by trade unions and management to agree on modifications to work patterns in a particular company	A decision by a large national company to change its product range
NATIONAL	A decision by a government committee to accept comment on a discussion document	A decision between management and trade unions in a particular industry to accept a new wage structure for the industry	A decision by Parliament to pass new legislation
INTER-NATIONAL	A decision by an international body to accept a particular subject for investigation	A decision by an international organization to allocate a large part of its budget to support a project in one country	A decision to build a fixed transport link between England and France across the English Channel
REGULATORY	A decision about whether a transgression of a particular rule should be taken to court	Decision about the introduction of new rules on the maximum radiation levels allowable	A decision about the acceptability of a site for a major new process plant

No discussion of the problems of decision making of the type that is in or close to the political arena is complete without drawing attention to the fact that such decisions are often one-off events in which there is little or no relevant quantified evidence to base the decision. This problem is returned to in several places in the study.

The conclusions that this examination of the problems of decision making warrant are: the range of sizes and complexity of decision making situations that exist is large. Although not discussed in detail the problem of being able to explain to others how, even simple, decisions were reached is recognized as being of vital importance. Inherent in explaining a decision is the problem of defining the basis for the decision and the weight that has to be given to the various factors and these aspects are explored in the chapters that follow. It is appreciated that it may not be possible to explain the significance of every factor to the same degree of accuracy, particularly when novel features are involved.

Also in the chapters that follow it is shown how the consistent basis for decision making provided by the Ranking Technique goes some way towards solving the problem of making decisions more easily explainable and defensible.

Chapter 3

The Relevance of Decision Analysis
Techniques Currently Available

In the general sense decision making involves determining the optimum
course of action to achieve a particular goal. Before any analysis
can start the goal or objective must be defined. In the context of
this study the goals may range from determining the acceptability of a
proposed site for a nuclear power station to determining the
acceptability of risk for insurance purposes. In other words the
techniques discussed are and indeed must be suitable for a very wide
range of applications. Decision analysis involves evaluating the
evidence available and determining what is likely to be the most
efficacious way of achieving the objective set. In this assessment of
the potency of the various decision analysis techniques, the general
nature of the techniques is first assessed, then their strengths and
weaknesses are examined.

The techniques that are considered are: payoff and other matrices,
decision trees, utility, risk reduction method, the Hurwicz Criterion,
the principle of insufficient reason, investment decisions under risk
and uncertainty, politometric multi-variate models and fuzzy logic.

Payoff matrices are generally built up by constructing a matrix of
strategies for dealing with all possible related events or situations,
the optimum solution being found by evaluating the matrix constructed
against a criterion that identifies the objective set of the
particular case. Typically the criterion used may be: the best
payoff strategy, the best average payoff strategy or the best expected
value strategy. Some of the criteria used make no allowance for the
probability of the events involved, but the best expected value
criterion weights each strategy considered according to its
probability. If quantitative data is not available the matrix may
also be built up in a way that incorporates only qualitative
assessments of the possible outcomes of the various strategies.

Matrices have the merit that they structure the analysis of the
different combinations of events and strategies that are considered
possible. It is the fact that various possible outcomes are
considered that is the main attraction of the technique, as it is a
way of allowing for uncertainty about the evidence. All the possible
combinations of events and strategies may not be realistic. Also the
data used may not be relevant or reliable. When a complex decision
situation has to be analysed the matrix may become very large and
cumbersome. The fact that the data may not be reliable and the
analysis becomes cumbersome when complex systems have to be analysed
is true of most decision analysis techniques when they are applied in
real life to major projects. One way matrix presentation may be
exploited to display the results of a Ranking of decision options is
specifically dealt with in Chapter 10.

Decision trees can in some ways be regarded as a way of demonstrating the way the various alternatives develop in complex decision issues. Generally decision trees show how the strategic decisions and events are linked to the various possible payoffs. The term "payoff" being used to denote the final result of a series of linked events in units appropriate to the particular decision being analysed. Construction of a decision tree does by its very nature expose critical points and where alternatives may be needed. Decision trees are subject to the same caveats as matrices with regard to: the accuracy of the data used, the possibility of making the assessment in qualitative terms and the method becoming cumbersome when complex systems are analysed. Developments of the decision tree technique that are related to specific forms of decision analysis are Probabilistic Safety Assessment (PSA) and Probabilistic Risk Assessment (PRA). PSA being aimed at the evaluation of plant reliability and the consequence of failure and PRA being aimed specifically at evaluation of the risk associated with a plant.

In evaluating decision options either by matrices or decision trees it has been shown that the optimum strategy can be identified in terms of the probability of some form of payoff. However, payoff in terms of utility function analysis has sometimes been described as a way of taking account of the decision maker's attitude to risk.[5] Because utility concepts were initially developed for economic analysis, utility is often expected to be related to financial variables but other units can be used. As conventionally used an arbitrary scale of utility is established, say from -10 to +10. Against this scale the other variables of the decision problem can be judged. The other variable may be the magnitude of a hazard, the degree of environmental pollution, the return on an investment, the cost of a project, the rate of expansion of an organization or the premiums people are willing to pay to cover against certain risks. Constructing a utility function does require the decision maker to assess what is the acceptability of the probability of possible outcomes from the proposal being evaluated, so the utility function does contain an element of probability in it. The assessment of acceptability will be different for different people and different in different circumstances. A banker's view of the utility of a particular investment may be quite different to that of a film producer or a government department. Most researchers know how difficult it is to find funding for major novel projects, which illustrates the view of some financiers on the utility of research. Utility is then a way of the decision maker expressing his assessment of acceptability of the various options available.

One aid to decision making that has been used in the nuclear industry in the United States of America is the Risk Reduction Method described by Vesely and Davis in reference 10. The method they describe is simply based on rating the technical aspects of risk, so makes no attempt at comprehensive assessment covering economic and socio-political factors involved in the decision. The method has been used to assess the relative merits of various possible alterations to reactor systems to determine which alteration will give the biggest benefit in risk reduction. There is nothing about the method that makes it peculiar to the nuclear industry, the method can be applied to comparison of any technical issue provided an appropriate assessment is available. The essential feature of the method is to compare benefits of possible action in technical terms of risk achievement worth and risk reduction worth. The two terms are most easily understood from the algebraic description of their definitions.

Risk Achievement Worth Ratio A = $\frac{Ri}{Ro}$

where Ro = present risk level
Ri = risk level with feature of interest
failed or removed

Risk Reduction Worth Ratio R = $\frac{Ro}{Rp}$

where Rp = risk level with feature of interest
optimized or made perfectly reliable

The risk achievement worth ratio gives a measure of the worth of a feature in achieving the present risk level. The risk reduction worth ratio gives a measure of the worth of a feature in reducing the level or risk further. The merit claimed for the method is that it helps the decision maker by rating the technical significance of the option without changing the logic of the assessment required.

The problem that remains is on what basis should the decision maker judge acceptability.   A partial answer to this question is given by the Hurwicz Criterion.[3][6] The Hurwicz Criterion suggests that the decision maker should base his decision on a weighted average of the smallest and largest payoffs of each alternative strategy. The weighting being a matter of the decision maker's judgement, a pessimistic decision maker might give more weight to the possibility of small payoffs, but an optimistic decision maker might give most weight to the possibility of a large payoff. The Hurwicz Criterion leaves many aspects of decision making still to be resolved. It could almost be described as introducing a qualitative element into a quantitative assessment.

The principle of insufficient reason is another attempt to find a universal comprehensive answer to decision making problems. The principle states: if, for a mutually exclusive and exhaustive listing of states of nature S_1, S_2......S_n there is no evidence to suggest that one state is more likely than another, we may take them all as equally probable.[6] Thus, a probability of 1/n can be assigned to each state. This transforms the decision problem under uncertainty to being one under risk.   The utility of each decision option A_x being $1/n \sum_1^n U$ where U represents the various components of utility of the particular option. The decision about which alternative to accept being made by selecting the alternative with the highest expected utility. Again it can be seen that the method is not a complete and comprehensive evaluation of all the factors involved in decision making. The method may be biased by the decision maker's choice of utility defining parameter and the approach may be considered inadequate if the list of options is incomplete. Incomplete listing of options is a possible weakness of many techniques.

As the list of techniques considered grows it becomes clearer that one very important central issue is the reliablity of the estimates of the risks and uncertainty. The question of the value of probability that should be used in assessing investment decisions under risk and uncertainty has been considered at length by Koutsoyiannis.[3] The arguments Koutsoyiannis used are equally applicable to any decision making situation.

The point that is particularly relevant to the purpose of this study is that all the techniques for decision making under uncertainty involve, in some form, doubts about the value of probability that should be used. The approach to evaluating the value of probability can be either objective or subjective. In the objective approach the estimate of probability is by definition based to some extent on past experience and in the subjective approach the estimate of probability is based on the decision maker's belief or confidence in a particular outcome. The main criticism of objective estimates is that they may be using past data that is not really relevant to the future conditions being considered. For some decisions the subjective approach may be superior to the objective approach particularly when it takes into account both historical data and the decision maker's assessment of the various factors that are likely to influence the value of probability under the circumstances being considered. In such cases it is a requirement that the decision maker has either relevant experience, or is advised by someone who has relevant experience, of the subject of the decision and arrives at his judgement in an impartial way free from bias.

Politometric multivariate modelling and fuzzy logic analysis are methods that attempt to deal with the decisions involving many uncertain variables. Gordon Hilton gave a good introduction to the politometric multi-variate approach in reference 7. The essential feature of the approach is the construction of a system of equations which describe the position that the various groups party to a particular decision adopt on that decision. It may be that some groups only have views on one component of the decision. For example, they may only have views on the technical factors or the socio-political factors. The views may be those of experts on some related aspect of the issue. Ideally equations should include an error term to allow for uncertainty and errors in the data that have to be used to solve the equation. Also the equation should be combined in a way that allows for feedback between the various components of the system.[9] The system of equations built up should include as many as possible of the variables associated with the decision being considered. Arriving at a decision about the optimum way a demand could be satisfied requires detailed analysis of the related equations and also an estimate of the rewards that would result from satisfying the demand. It is implicit in such an analysis that there is a time element in the system of equations. If the data available to solve such equations are near perfect such a solution would be very helpful, but the size of the error function in practical cases is likely to reduce the solution to general guidance. This problem of dealing with the fuzziness of the data has led to the development of the fuzzy logic approach. It is appreciated that the fuzzy logic approach is a relatively new mathematical technique and one that is still developing.*

The concept of fuzzy logic was developed as part of the process of developing computers with artificial intelligence.[11] One form of this artificial intelligence can write a precis of a typical news event by using scripts stored in the computer's memory.[12] For example, in describing the consequences of an earthquake the computer would attempt to bring together details of the magnitude of: the fault, the damage, the homeless, the injured and those killed. Although there is some argument that fuzzy logic is just a restatement of probability, it has been put to practical uses including even the control of cement-kilns.[11] In the past cement-kilns were controlled by operators who had learned by experience how to interpret for control purposes the limited measurements that are possible about conditions inside the kiln. By determining how operators would respond to various conditions such as lime content and kiln drive torque fuzzy logic curves were constructed. By incorporating these curves into a control microprocessor the kilns can be controlled automatically as efficiently as they could be by the original human operators. Other applications of the fuzzy logic processing that are being considered are in assessing company profit margins, driving trains and guiding robot arc-welders.

Fuzzy logic can be used to assess the extent to which any target is being or will be satisfied. The possibility of using the fuzzy logic approach to assess the degree of compliance with safety goals that would be acceptable has been considered.[13] Among the advantages that are claimed for the method are that it is a logical disciplined technique, it allows for the uncertainty and vagueness in the data available and it can be used in a way that can incorporate technical, economic and socio-political factors. The view has been expressed that the disadvantages of the method, which stem mainly from the general unfamiliarity of the method, will be overcome. The application of fuzzy analysis is considered further in Chapter 10.

---

*For anyone interested in a more detailed understanding of fuzzy logic the following references will be useful:-
1)   HORSAK R.D. and DAMICO S.A. Risk Evaluation of Hazardous Waste Disposal Sites using Fuzzy Set Analysis published in Risk Assessment and Management edited by Love L.B. published by Plenum Press, New York 1987, pp 643-648.
2)   PREYSSL C. "Fuzzy Risk" Analysis Theory and Application published by International Institute for Applied System Analysis, Laxenburg, Austria, 1986.
3)   COOK I., UNWIN S.E. NUREG/CR-4514 Controlling Principles for Prior Probablity Assignments in Nuclear Risk Assessment, published by the U.S. Nuclear Regulatory Commission, 1986.
4)   CATTANEO F., DeSANTIS S., GARRIBA S.G., VOLTA G. Learning from Abnormal Occurences: Results of a Fuzzy Analysis, a paper presented at the PSA '87 Conference, Zurich 1987.
5)   UNWIN S.D. Fuzzy Set theoretic foundation for use in uncertainty analysis, Risk Analysis Vol. 6 No. 1 1986, published by the Plenum Publishing Corporation, New York.

Returning now to the general question of the relevance of decision making techniques to large comprehensive decisions, such as government approval of the siting of a nuclear power station or a potentially hazardous chemical works. The important characteristic required of procedures is that they are able to take into account the interests and influences of many factors and organizations.[8] For a decision procedure to give a satisfactory comprehensive assessment of the options it must include assessment of the following issues:-

1) The technical and economic nature and implications of the proposal being considered.
2) The views of the people likely to be affected by the decision.
3) The acceptability of the various options should be conducted in terms that are fully understandable by all involved.

That this list of requirements confirms the view that for a decision process to be effective in the comprehensive sense it must take into account in a consistent way the technical, economic and socio-political nature and implications of the proposal being considered. For any process to be effective the purpose of the proposal being evaluated for a decision must be clearly defined and any uncertainties in the data that has to be used identified in a way that is defensible and explainable.

The conclusions that seem to be justified about other aids to decision making are: 1) None of the analysis techniques considered attempts to consider all the factors involved in the comprehensive way that the Risk Ranking Technique does, but the techniques can be useful for assessing the evidence for Ranking. 2) The techniques alone do not identify what is acceptable, they leave it to the decision maker to decide the criteria he will use to judge acceptability. 3) Techniques exist for allowing for uncertainty in the data that has to be used. 4) There is considerable scope for improving the presentation of the results of decision analysis. The results should be presented in a way that makes their significance clear in a simple and unambiguous way. 5) Ideally both the decision making analysis techniques and the circumstances under which they are used should match, but such an ideal is difficult to achieve. The problem is to identify the most efficient decision making procedure. (The way the Ranking Technique can be used to solve this problem is discussed further in Chapter 10).

Chapter 4
The Nature of the Ranking Technique

In this chapter the aims of the Risk Ranking Technique and the way the Technique is designed to satisfy these aims are examined. The main aim of the Technique is to provide the decision maker with a unified, consistent, comprehensive and defensible assessment of the acceptability of the various decision options.

To rank the acceptability of the various options the Technique integrates the acceptability of the technical, economic and socio-political factors associated with each option. These three factors are intended to cover the whole spectrum of features that are involved. In table 4 some possible compositions of the three factors are shown. It is stressed that the table only describes possible compositions of the factors and the precise composition used must be tailored to suit the particular nature of the decision concerned. The procedure for scoring the acceptability of the individual factors and arriving at a comprehensive ranking of acceptability is summarized in Appendix 1.

In designing the Technique, the three groups of factors were taken through to the final stage of the assessment to show clearly that they have been considered thoroughly in arriving at a comprehensive assessment of acceptability. The assumption being that no adequately justified decision could be made simply on the attractiveness of one factor and any real balanced decision, particularly when it is related to a major complex proposal, would have to be based on assessment of the merits, interactions and weighting of all the factors concerned. The design intention being to make clear the basis on which the ranking given to the acceptability of each factor can be defended.

One step back from Ranking the acceptability is establishing the criteria for judging the significance of each factor. Also the relevance and reliability of the data that has to be used has to be evaluated. Most of the discussion in this Chapter and Chapters 5, 6 and 7 is related to the situation when some quantitative data is available. In many real life decision making situations there is only qualitative data available and this situation is discussed in Chapters 9 and 10.

The effectiveness of any assessment depends on the quality of the evidence available. The world stock of data is enormous, there are data banks and statistical reports on almost every subject. One very usual problem is that the data is often published in a form that suggests they are authoritative and trustworthy, but they are often riddled with various types of errors. The three main types of error are: sampling, measurement and reliability errors. In the following a pragmatic approach to dealing with errors is developed and not a novel theoretical approach.

TABLE 4   COMPOSITION OF THE MAIN GROUPS OF RANKING FACTORS

FACTOR	NATURE OF RISK	POSSIBLE COMPOSITIONS OF FACTORS
TECHNICAL	Degree of physical harm to people and property.	Plant reliability, Societal risk. Individual risk. Comparison with other risks.
ECONOMIC	Less than optimum benefit from financial commitment.	Supply and demand. Value of life. Cost of saving life. Marginal cost of saving a life. Payoff. Index of harm/benefit. Cost/benefit analysis.
SOCIO-POLITICAL	Public opposition.	Public acceptability. Results of Public Inquiries. Political climate. Views on current quality of life.

The population from which the data is derived may not really be uniform. In the case of engineering components or systems, members of the population may perform similar functions, but be made in very different ways. Additionally data may have been collected on a quota basis, which reflects assumed traits of the population and so introduces bias. When the population is large and the sample is large both the law of large numbers and the central limit theorem help to determine the significance of the data. The law of large numbers states that with a large number of samples the mean of the sample means will equal the mean of the population. The central limit theorem states that if we draw numerous large samples the means of the samples will approximate a normal distribution. Even if the sampling technique is perfect the errors in the population used have to be considered.

A few examples illustrate quite clearly the significance of these errors. In the technical field typical population errors which can occur are those that arise when faults are predicted in components that are operating in quite different environments to those in which the fault data was collected. For example, data on the failure rate of temperature trips in high temperature chemical systems may be required, but the only data population that exists is for trips used in high speed aircraft gas turbines. Even apart from the difference in operating environment in the example cited there would be differences in design, specification and quality control that the two populations of trips are subject to.

Population differences related to economic data are also quite dramatic. The differences between nations are particularly significant. For example, the value of life is particularly prone to differences in culture and national preferences. This illustrates the importance of the economic data used being drawn from a population similar to the population the data is to be used to characterize.

Sources of errors in socio-political data populations are many and various. Socio-political data is intimately related to the views and reactions of people. It is therefore essential that the population data used is from the same population to which the analysis will be applied. This requirement applies down to very local levels where for example the views of people in one part of a city may be different from those in another part.

The conclusion that is justified about the way sampling errors may be minimized is that the population of data from which the data is drawn must be similar to that to which the data is to be applied and the sample of data analysed must be drawn in an unbiased way.

The errors in measurement take four main forms which are: errors in concepts of data, errors due to changing circumstances, errors in data transformations and errors due to lack of data points. Errors of concept are essentially related to the way the data required is defined. It may be that the data required is defined too loosely. For example, the data required may be defined as bridge failures, which is a very general term as there are many different types of bridges; if the bridges of interest are suspension bridges the failure rates of wooden bridges are unlikely to be relevant. The obvious way of overcoming this problem is to check that the data required is correctly specified and that the data used matches the specification.

Changing circumstances are the cause of an important class of errors. For example engineering components may be made from different materials or manufactured in different ways, both types of change may radically affect their performance and reliability. Economic factors are particularly subject to changing circumstances. Changes in supply and demand, inflation, interest rates and financial restrictions are just a few of the aspects of economic factors that can change and for which proper allowance has to be made. Economic data collected only a year or two ago is bound to need adjustment for the factors just mentioned and such adjustments introduce errors. If the data is older the corrections are likely to be even more doubtful. Also the economic data collected in one country is unlikely to be exactly relevant to another country without considerable correction. Socio-political factors are also subject to change with time, the way such factors may change is dramatically illustrated by the changes that elections produce in the political party in power. The socio-political factors are perhaps the most difficult to correct for changes that take place with time.

Errors in transformations are really errors in the corrections made to change data collected in one set of circumstances to be applicable to different circumstances. This means that transformation errors are very similar to the errors due to changing circumstances, which have just been discussed.

When the data does not extend over the required range the problem is often overcome by extrapolation, this gives rise to lack of data point errors, the error being related to the extent to which the extrapolation used can be justified.

The conclusion that seems to be warranted about the action that should be taken to minimize measurement errors is that care must be taken to check that the data used does not contain errors due to: wrong concepts of data, errors resulting from changing circumstances, errors due to inappropriate transformations and errors due to lack of data points. This conclusion really amounts to a data check procedure. The essential steps required to reduce errors in data are formalised in Table 5. If the steps in the data check procedure outlined are followed a much greater understanding of the confidence that can be placed in the data will be established. It is important to notice that it is only claimed the error can be minimized and no claim is made that the errors can be eliminated. This means there are likely to be errors in any data used to evaluate decision options.

Ideally the Ranking Technique requires a quantitative assessment of the related technical, economic and socio-political factors, but the technique may be used when only qualitative data is available. If qualitative data have to be used it is even more important that the precautions just described for quantitative data are observed. Simply collecting the relevant data in a structured way and subjecting it to a critical examination exposes its quality and the reliance that can be placed on it for decision making.

The Ranks defined by the Technique serve two vital purposes, they grade the acceptability of each factor in absolute terms and the width of each Rank gives a measure of the uncertainty associated with each factor. Relating the width of each Rank to the inherent uncertainty is an attractive feature of the Technique.

TABLE 5   SUMMARY OF PRECAUTIONS TO REDUCE ERRORS IN DATA USED

CATEGORY OF ERROR	NATURE OF ERROR	STEP IN PUBLISHED DATA ANALYSIS TO IDENTIFY AND ATTENUATE ERROR
SAMPLING	POPULATION FROM WHICH SAMPLE IS DRAWN	Check that the population from which the data are drawn is similar to which the data are to be applied
	WAY IN WHICH SAMPLE IS DRAWN	Design the sampling so that it represents a random sample of the population, if this is not possible determine the magnitude of the error involved
MEASUREMENT	CONCEPT OF DATA	Check that the data use matches the specification of the data to be obtained
	CHANGING CIRCUMSTANCES	Check that the circumstances and environment surrounding the data when it was collected match the circumstances and environment surrounding the use of the data
	TRANSFOR-MATIONS	Determine the significance and appropriateness of any corrections made to the data
	LACK OF POINTS	Assess the suitability of any extrapolation made to be the data used to enable it to fit the required range
RELIABILITY	DATA COLLECTION	Assess the data collection process to determine the nature and extent of any errors that may have been built into the system
	DATA PROCESSING	Assess the way the data has been processed to determine the nature and extent of any errors that may have been made

Chapter 5

Evaluation of Technical Factors for Ranking

To provide a basis for the examination of the criteria for scoring
Technical Factors for Ranking the first part of this chapter is
devoted to defining the nature of Technical Factors in more detail.
To help relate the definition to the process of Ranking a model is
presented which illustrates the nature of the factors and the way they
may interact to influence one another. Using the model as a base, in
the second part of the chapter the scoring for Ranking acceptability
of technical factors is evaluated. The final part of the chapter
summarizes the conclusions that appear to be justified about the
considerations that should be taken into account in the development of
coherent and consistent criteria for scoring the risk acceptability
of technical factor.

NATURE OF TECHNICAL FACTORS

Obviously the spectrum of factors that could be considered is very
wide and the first question is how can the spectrum be refined to
focus attention on the factors of direct interest. The spectrum of
factors to be considered is to some extent defined by the use the
Ranking Technique is to be put to. Although the Technique can be used
for many purposes from assessing research project decision options to
assessing major construction projects like the Channel Tunnel
attention is concentrated on assessing the acceptability of the risks
associated with major novel projects. To help explain the nature of
the factors a model has been constructed which contains the four
essential elements of all technical factors. The central feature of
the model is the source term, which may be single or multi-variable in
nature. A factor with a single source term is one that has only one
form of risk associated with it. Such a factor would be very simple.
In real life single source term factors are likely to be very rare and
factors with multi-variable source terms are more usual. Clearly the
source term must contain all the variables necessary to define the
characteristics of all the components of the source term. The second
essential feature of the model is the control element it incorporates,
which is intended to represent all the measures that are included in
the proposal being evaluated with the aim of keeping the subject of
the proposal within specification. The third essential feature of the
model is the containment element, which represents the measures
incorporated with the objective of limiting the external consequences
of undesirable events. Outside the containment element is the fourth
feature, the environment which represents all those features of the
real world which surround every factor and may alter them or be
altered by them. In figure 3 the idealized model of a technical
factor is shown diagrammatically in its simplest form just as a factor
operating in a universal environment.

In reality technical factors are very complex and normally involve a
network of interacting components, the interactions generally being
non-linear and multi-directional. Analysis of such complex networks

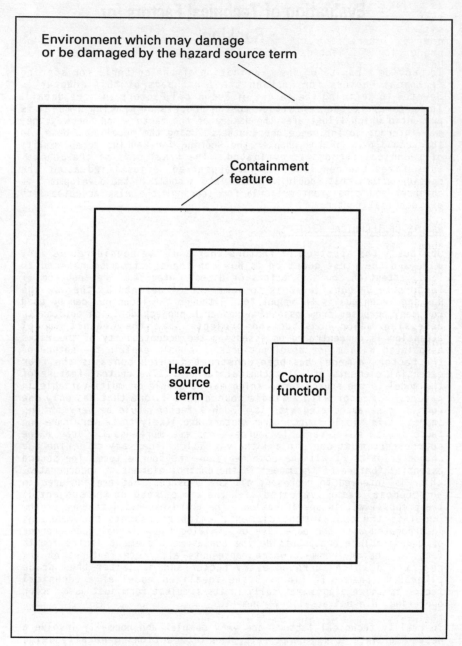

Environment which may damage
or be damaged by the hazard source term

Containment
feature

Hazard
source
term

Control
function

Fig 3 Model of a potentially hazardous system

is difficult but not impossible, as already mentioned, techniques have even been developed for analysis of political systems. Political systems are very difficult to analyse because they contain many complex interacting and difficult to predict variables, a large proportion of which can only be described in qualitative terms.[7] Unique situations may have to be considered for which relevant quantitative data does not exist nor will it be generated in the one-off situation. It may be with such a lack of data the most that can be hoped for is development of a vector giving an indication of the direction and magnitude of the reliability that can be associated with the factor's performance.

Having drawn attention to the complex nature of the elements that make up a technical factor the evaluation of such factors can be discussed.

EVALUATION OF TECHNICAL FACTORS

Before embarking on a discussion of the evaluation of various technical Ranking factors their potential significance has to be put into perspective. It has to be recognized that generally judgements about the acceptability of various factors have to be refined iteratively as a project develops. This is particularly true when a project is novel and there are few or no relevant data to base judgements on. At each decision stage judgements have to be made about the adequacy of the justification of the development of the relevant arguments. Determination of the overall acceptability of a major project such as a power plant or a new aeroplane requires the collection and evaluation of an enormous amount of evidence and the integration of analyses of many subsystems.

At each stage of a project attention is focused on different aspects of the decision and often different people are involved with justifying and judging acceptability. Some specific examples of technical acceptability criteria are given in Appendix 3. For example the designer has to decide what he will submit for approval at the various stages to demonstrate that his design satisfies all the relevant criteria or at least is making progress towards satisfying them. The demonstration may include showing, as appropriate, how: stresses in structural members will be kept below those allowed by current Codes of Practice, loads on foundations will be kept below the maximum allowed by local soil and rock conditions, pressurized equipment is designed to satisfy legal and insurance requirements and electrical equipment will be designed and installed to conform with the relevant electrical regulations. Demonstration that criteria have been satisfied may in some cases be facilitated by the use of Probabilistic Safety Assessments (PSA) or Probabilistic Risk Assessments (PRA). Also at the design stage care must be taken to ensure, as far as possible, that the design satisfies all planning requirements. This may include demonstrating that the design satisfies aesthetic requirements and environmental requirements such as all possible discharges to the atmosphere of potentially hazardous materials will be within specified limits.

Proving criteria are satisfied is of equal interest to official regulatory bodies and owners. The concern of owners being to ensure that the proposal they are putting forward will not involve them in unexpected liability and to ensure that official criteria are properly and quickly satisfied. Owners want to avoid delays in the product of their investment being brought into productive operation, so wish to keep possible causes of delays to a minimum. For similar reasons, owners or proposers will maintain contact with regulatory bodies in an attempt to agree criteria and the way they can be interpreted so that the design can be made to satisfy all acceptability requirements in a consistent way.

This demonstrates that the most effective criteria are likely to be those that specify the conditions that have to be satisfied in comprehensive terms that cover all the circumstances involved. It does not mean that the requirements have to described in vague qualitative terms although there may sometimes be merit in using qualitative terms.

In most European countries the primary legislation for control of potentially hazardous installations does not specify the technical acceptability of a potential risk in probability terms.[14] Although there are several forms of frequency/harm limit lines, which are in various ways being used to guide judgements about acceptability. Among these limit lines are: the French nuclear reactor design objectives, the United Kingdom and German assessment levels and the Dutch threshold values for acceptability.[15][16] The way requirements for hazardous installations are specified in several European countries is summarized in Table 6. In industrial countries, apart from the Netherlands, quantitative limit line acceptability criteria for potentially hazardous installations have not been adopted for general application. In the USA[17] the USNRC have issued a policy statement containing risk acceptability criteria for nuclear plant, but this is not based on the broader national acceptance of the criteria as, for example, the ALARP principle adopted in the UK. It is interesting to note that the USNRC chose to express their risk criteria for nuclear plant as a fraction of existing risks, rather than in absolute terms. A summary of the USNRC policy statement is given in Appendix 4, which shows how in this particular case goals for acceptable individual risk and social risk are stated in both qualitative and quantitative terms.

If technical requirements are only specified in qualitative terms two main types of problem are generated, they are: 1) The proposer does not have a precisely defined numerical requirement to satisfy. 2) When there is no quantitative target to satisfy, proof that a proposal is acceptable is a matter of judgement. It therefore follows that if any claim is made against an owner of plant or equipment whose acceptability is justified simply in qualitative technical terms, there may be difficulty in proving that all that is reasonably practicable has been done to make the plant or equipment acceptable, and that the likelihood of any accident with unacceptable consequences had been reduced as far as is reasonably practicable.[18]

The problems involved in deciding what is acceptable are considerably easier to solve when the nature of any intrinsic hazard is known completely. However, in reality new projects generally bring in their

TABLE 6 SUMMARY OF RISK ACCEPTABILITY CRITERIA
         IN SEVERAL COUNTRIES

COUNTRY	LEGAL TERMS USED DEFINE ACCEPTABILITY	OUTLINE OF JUSTIFICATION REQUIRED	USE MADE OF QUANTIFICATION OF RISK
GERMANY	"Generally approved technical rules" subject to licensing if they cause "harmful effects" or "cause considerable disadvantage".	Safety analysis required. Latest stage of technology.	Only as part of the safety analysis. There are no quantified targets to be satisfied.
BRITAIN	Precautions should be as "the best practical means" and the risk "as low as reasonably achievable."	Hazard survey based on form of quantitative assessment. May be subject to Public Inquiry	It has been suggested that a risk of a serious accident of 1×10^{-4} year is on the borderline of acceptability.[19]
FRANCE	Plant requires authorization if material is on the official list and is above the threshold value.	A risk assessment and an environmental impact statement.	To quantify consequences. Risk of an unacceptable consequence should not exceed 1×10^{-6}/yr. This is a guide rather than a mandatory limit.
DENMARK	Legal requirements expressed in general terms. Importance attached to project being acceptable to Safety Committee of the Undertaking.	To show environmental contamination not above threshold values and pressurized components are properly designed.	50 installations identified as potentially hazardous and requiring assessment. Risk of a person being killed of 1×10^{-6}/yr has been accepted.
NETHER-LANDS	Safety report required if accident would seriously endanger life 100m away. For the plant with the highest hazard potential probability must be quantified as accurately as possible.	Safety report approved by regulatory authorities and Works Council. Suitability of operating staff must be assessed.	Analysis in term of: probability, and indices of fire explosion and toxicity. Provisional maximum acceptable individual risk of death 1×10^{-6} per year.

train new hazards that are not fully understood, so some way of judging acceptability has to be found for proposals that are novel. It may be that for such cases an element of qualitative judgement must be retained in the criteria or it is overtly accepted that justification may be substantiated by a specially designed research and development programme. Obvious examples of this approach are the prototype testing of new designs of aeroplanes and motor cars.

If the acceptability of a project has to be defended publicly, quantitative evidence about the technical nature and level of risk involved will create confidence that at least the risk is understood. When such evidence is not available the impression will be created that the proposer does not properly understand the implications of his submission. In other words the absence of quantitative evidence will suggest that the understanding of the risks associated with a proposal is incomplete. Something of the nature of the process of justifying to regulatory authorities that a complex project is acceptable is given by the steps the Central Electricity Generating Board expect a nuclear reactor proposal to go through to obtain an operating licence, which are described in Appendix 5. Merely expressing the risk in quantitative terms does not answer all the questions. For a quantitative statement to be acceptable the adequacy of the data used must, as discussed in Chapter 4, be understood.

Provided a quantitative statement can be based on appropriate reliable data it is more informative than a qualitative statement, as it gives a factual indication of the significance of the risk. It is therefore logical to aim to have compliance with technical risk acceptability criteria substantiated in quantitative terms. This leads immediately to the question of what units should technical criteria be defined in.

There are several units that could be used, most obvious candidates are time and fatalities, as these indicate in a very direct way the ultimate harm to the people involved in a particular unit of time. An alternative would be to define the risk in money terms, which is very much the approach of an insurance underwriter. It is appreciated that for several applications money may be the appropriate unit. There can, however, be some doubt about what is included in the monetary equivalent of a risk. Equally, even describing a risk simply in terms of the number of fatalities is ambiguous, as it would not include non-fatal casualties or give a direct indication of material damage. Also it involves problems of attributing monetary values to events and expressing costs in a common currency, which may change in value. It is worth noting that there has been some public opposition to basing risk acceptability decisions on monetary criteria in the form of cost-benefit analysis.[20] The central difficulty that remains is how to compare fairly the technical risk associated with different proposals that have dramatically different characteristics. For example chemicals can have as significant but different effect as radiation.[21] Perhaps all that need be said at this stage, is that when comparisons of risk are made they should be made in consistent units, but it is recognized that it may prove exceedingly difficult to obtain agreement about what these units should be.

Perhaps the most important characteristics required of criteria for assessing acceptability of technical factors are that they should be easily understandable and interpretable. This may sound trite but it is fundamental, because unless everyone at risk can understand and discuss the meaning of the criteria there will be no general confidence in their adequacy. Next, criteria must have clearly defined limits of application. For example if the criteria are aimed at ensuring the risks associated with chemical plants are acceptable the criteria must state clearly whether they apply to chemical plants for the manufacture of all chemicals or just to some chemicals. Similarly if the criteria are intended to be universal it should be stated clearly that they are intended to ensure the same level of risk regardless of the activity considered. Sometimes risks are divided into direct and indirect risks. Direct risks simply being damage and harm to people and plant directly involved in the activity concerned. Indirect risks are all the other possible consequential losses like: loss of production, damage to people outside the site and loss of customers. Total risks are the sum of direct and indirect risks. A comprehensive criteria should be based on the total potential risk that could be associated with the proposal. The criteria should specify the total limit to risk that must not be exceeded, as a result of the activity.

From the overall criteria partial criteria can be derived. Partial criteria being the criteria that the various subsystems of a plant or activity have to satisfy. The way partial criteria are defined depends to a very large extent on the form of the plant. The more complex the plant the more parts the overall criteria will have to be divided into. The important condition that must be satisfied is that the integrated risk from all the subsystems of the plant must still satisfy the overall criteria.

Provided overall criteria are used in the sense of a maximum spectrum of risk and not some kind of average risk the identification of partial criteria is logical. Although there may be discussion about the realistic allowance that has to be made for the intrinsic uncertainties.(22)

CRITERIA FOR RANKING TECHNICAL FACTORS

In table 6 and references 14 and 15 an indication is given of the current stage of development that criteria for judging the acceptability of potentially hazardous plant had reached in several countries. In general the status is that quantitative goals specifying acceptability in probabilistic terms are used in an indicative way simply to supplement the traditional deterministic approach, but there are differences between countries in the way goals are specified.

Ideally the criteria that are adopted should be equally applicable to all risks. There is no moral justification for treating the various types of imposed risk differently. It can well be envisaged that there are special circumstances when very much higher risks are considered to be justified: one case is when it would generally be agreed that higher risks are justified is when a surgeon takes a high risk in order to try and save or improve the quality of life. This is a very forceful way of introducing the nature of the risk-benefit argument. The risk/benefit options that have to be considered when the siting of a potentially hazardous plant has to be assessed are more subtle, and are considered later.

On the basis just outlined it is suggested that the overall technical risk acceptability criteria for determining Ranking could take the form shown in Table 7. The justification for suggesting the criteria should take the form described is that it combines the Ashby criteria and the Ranking Technique described in reference 3 and Appendix 1.

TABLE 7   PROPOSED TECHNICAL RISK ACCEPTABILITY CRITERIA

RISK RANK SCORE	ACCEPTABILITY	MEAN INDIVIDUAL RISK OF DEATH PER YEAR	COMMENTS
3-4	Unacceptable	Close to or greater than 1 in 1,000	The risk would have to be significantly reduced for it to become acceptable
2-3	Only acceptable under special circumstances	Of the order of: 1 in 10,000	In general the risk would have to be reduced to make it acceptable
1-2	Would require detailed evaluation to justify acceptability	Of the order of: 1 in 100,000	There would be particular concern if there was a chance of multiple fatalities
0-1	Acceptable without restriction	Close to or less than 1 in 1,000,000	There may be some reservations if there was a chance of multiple fatalities

Describing the criteria in this way defines the overall requirement that must be satisfied and is independent of the nature of the plant being considered. This means that any partial requirements, such as for the reliability of subsystems can be derived for a particular design from the overall requirement. In general the criteria that components or subsystems of complete projects should satisfy must be such that the risk associated with each of them will when integrated in an appropriated way be equal to or less than the risk allowed by the overall criteria for the whole installation.

Some confidence that the risk acceptability criteria proposed are of the right order is given by the Layfield report on the Sizewell 'B' Public Inquiry. In the report an estimated maximum individual risk of death for members of the public of one in three million per year was accepted.[23] This risk being made up of normal operation risk of 30×10^{-8}, design basis accidents risk of 4×10^{-8} and beyond design basis accident risk of 0.2×10^{-8}. This shows in practice how criteria for subsystems can be formed by sub-division of the overall criteria. The Layfield report also accepted a social risk for the whole of the United Kingdom of one death every five hundred years.[23]

It is therefore considered that criteria, of the form suggested, are suitable for assessing the Ranking of the overall technical acceptability of most risk situations when an element of hazard to human life is involved. It is assumed that in determining Ranking the ability of an installation to withstand all relevant hazards no matter whether they are internally or externally generated will have been included in the evaluation. Internally generated hazards being those generated within the plant itself and externally generated hazards being those caused by some agency external to the plant being considered. One question about the criteria that is returned to in Chapters 9 and 11 is the validity of using the individual risk of death as the criteria for Ranking acceptability. Also the criteria for determining technical acceptability in decision making where risk of harm to the population is not a critical parameter in the decision is also returned to.

Chapter 6
Evaluation of Economic Factors for Ranking

This discussion of economic factors starts by considering the relevant general economic arguments, then the specific problem of evaluation of economic factors for Ranking is examined and finally criteria for Ranking economic factors are proposed.

ECONOMIC ARGUMENTS

Ultimately in most forms of industrial activity supply is adjusted to demand. The growth of nuclear power can in part be attributed to the growth in demand for electrical power and doubts about supply based on other fuels. In Britain prior to the decision to adopt nuclear power, there had been a succession of oil crises and miners' strikes to generate doubts about other forms of fuel supply. This relationship was specifically emphasized in a British Government report, which stated that the introduction of nuclear power should lead to a reduction in the National Coal Board's investment programme.[24] Similarly the economics of investment in the construction and operation of any chemical plant or airliners has to be justified positively in terms of demand and supply.

No matter what form the risk takes its acceptability in economic terms can be evaluated in several ways. Most of these methods of evaluation contain an element of comparison or in economic terms opportunity cost. Among these methods are: cost of saving a life, economic viability of a project, cost of compensation, risk-benefit analysis and cost-benefit analysis. The strength and limitations of these methods are examined in detail in reference 25 and also later in this chapter.

With a free democratic society any decision must reflect the interests and wishes of those individuals affected by the decision. Implicated in decisions about the acceptability of risk is the fact that somewhere in the economic environment considered there has to be someone who is willing to pay for a reduction of risk. Equally if a higher risk is accepted somewhere there must be a benefit that is considered to offset the higher risk costs involved. Clearly a balancing of the options has to be performed. As with proving evidence that the technical criteria are satisfied the economic data used and the methods of analysis have to be proved to be relevant. If the requirement was simply to follow the Ranking of the technical aspects of acceptability, proposed in Chapter 5, decisions should be based on an evaluation of: deaths, total costs and probability.

However, such a simplification is not a satisfactory basis for a decision about acceptability, particularly when a major project is involved, as it does not do justice to the economic arguments. The underlying aim of a responsible decision maker must be to ensure that resources are allocated to their most beneficial uses. This means the costs of risks involved have to be explicitly weighed against the other benefits and costs of the project.[26]

For a completely satisfactory assessment of the economic aspects of the acceptability of risk the assessment has to include evaluation of the following features:-

1)   An evaluation of the total costs of the project.
2)   An evaluation in money terms of the various benefits associated with the project. (It is appreciated that all the benefits may not be quantified and that some parts of the assessment may have to be made in qualitative terms.)
3)   An assessment of the errors and uncertainties associated with the estimates of costs and benefits.
4)   An assessment of the economics of possible alternatives.
5)   A quantitative evaluation of the costs associated with the risks inherent in the project.
6)   An assessment of the costs associated with the risk inherent in alternative projects.

The range of elements that has to be considered can be related to the model used to demonstrate the nature of technical factors, described in Figure 3 Chapter 5, in the following way:-

1)   The source term represents total estimated cost of the proposal.
2)   The control function represents the actions that can be taken to ensure the total costs remain within the estimated range.
3)   The containment feature represents the ultimate limit to funds available.
4)   The environment feature represents the overall economic well being of the company, community or nation involved.

Finally an indication of the magnitude of the economic implications of risk in various fields is given by the following examples:-   In the criminal negligence case brought against the manufacturer of the Pinto car as a result of an accident involving a car of that type, which killed three teenagers, the manufacturer showed their risk-benefit analysis to justify their decision about a safety modification.   They argued that an $11 modification would save 6 lives, as sales of this model were expected to be 400,000 the total cost would be $4,400,000. They put the cash value of a fatality at $400,000 making the total benefit of making the modification $2,400,000, which is a negative benefit.[20]   Jones-Lee has argued that an average motorist in Britain would be willing to pay £15 for a 10% reduction in the risk of being involved in a fatal accident next year.[26]

Other assessments that help to complete the picture of the economic implications of risk are:-

1)   It has been suggested that the cost of accidents in the world's oil refinery business is about £10 million a year, so the benefits of reducing risk are obvious.[27]
2)   Wilson and Crouch have suggested that for the 45 activites they examined the benefit of saving one life would be between $100 and $1,000,000,000.[28]
3)   In the comparison of electricity generating costs presented at

the Sizewell 'B' Public Inquiry it was stated by CEGB that for particular economic evaluations the net effective cost (NEC) of supplying electricity from the Sizewell 'B' pressurized water reactor would be -£56/KWpa and that for the   same conditions the cost of electricity from a coal fired power station would be £28/KWpa.[29]   Net effective cost represents the net cost of supplying electricty from a new power station, and is equal to the cost of building and operating the station less savings in operating costs elsewhere in the power system. A negative NEC shows that additional costs of the new power station are outweighed by cost saving elsewhere in the system and that the new station would be cost-saving over its lifetime. CEGB considered that oil fired plant was no longer economically viable and that renewable energy sources would not be practicable before the year 2000.   Although Layfield accepted that Sizewell 'B' was likely to be the least cost choice, the Public Inquiry showed clearly the uncertainty associated with the evidence on which economic arguments have to be based.

4)   In the Layfield report it was menionted that £1 million is towards the higher end of the suggested values of a life and that it would be difficult to justify spending more than an additional £500,000 to reduce further the risk to the public.[30]

EVALUATION OF ECONOMIC FACTORS

Evaluating the value of a life is complicated by the fact that there are several ways of valuing life, and even considerable debate about whether or not it is ethical to evaluate the value of life in money terms at all.[20][31]   It is important to understand the ethical argument as it puts into proper perspective discussion about the need to value human life carefully.

The central feature of the argument is how to decide what is an equitable distribution of risks and benefits in society. The two extremes of the argument are: it is unreasonable to expose anyone to any risk if they will not be compensated for any harm they suffer as a result of such exposure, and that provided the arrangements for compensation are adequate the risk will be acceptable. Both extremes of the argument are unreasonable and in most decisions some middle ground is found. Certainly nobody would be able to accept unlimited financial responsibility for risks and not many people would accept exposure to unlimited risk. These obvious limits to financial responsibility are important justifications for careful determination of the value ascribed to human life. Most organisations try to limit their liability in some way, but they do not buy unlimited insurance cover.[32] A word of warning must also be sounded about the use of the phrase 'careful determination of the value ascribed to human life'. The term 'value of human life' is often used as a surrogate for the impact of hazards on society. This is to oversimplify the argument and to imply actual values for the cultural significance of the sociological overtones of the factor. It is not intended to give the impression that cost benefit analysis, or any of the related techniques, can be made into precision tools. At best, risk benefit analysis or cost benefit analysis can only be used to make broad comparisons of risks. However, a broad rather coarse comparison is better than none.

Another important facet of the argument is the question 'Who bears the costs and who bears the benefits associated with the activity?' The argument is fairly simple when the costs and benefits are borne by the same party. But when the costs are borne by one party and the benefits by another party there is a deep moral question about how the benefits and burdens should be distributed. The following quotation from a Congressional Hearing goes some way towards identifying a solution to the problem in a way that helps to keep the discussion in this book about the value of human life in perspective.[31]

> 'The first moral question to be asked is this : "How ought benefits and risks be distributed?" It is a good rule of thumb to assume that no policy based directly on risk-benefit analysis will automaticaly distribute benefits and burdens fairly. That will happen only as the result of a deliberate additional effort. A very heavy burden of risk on one group, while another group gains most of the benefits, is clearly inequitable....'

The deduction that seems obvious from the above quotation is that the risk and benefits must be expressed in quantified terms to enable the equity of their distribution to be checked. It is only when the discussion can be held in numerical terms that the adequacy and fairness of the arrangements for compensation can be judged. Considering specifically the question of the value of human life, the extreme limits on the value are easily identified. Some people would argue that the value is infinite and others would argue that it is negligible. These extreme limits are often stated simply for bargaining purposes.

Those that argue that life is priceless would effectively stop all development, as it would be impossible to arrange compensation for a single victim of the development. Equally, if no value is ascribed to human life, it could encourage risky or life threatening developments to be accepted. Obviously between these limits is a value of human life that the decision maker could realistically use in his calculations of what is acceptable. Given that a precise value of human life is an unrealistic goal, the next step is to identify a value that gives the decision maker a practical guide to what is likely to be acceptable in the real world.

Valuation of lives for various economic purposes has a long history - in 1699 Sir William Petty valued an adult life at £160.[33] In 1864 the valuation of human capital was expressed in the following terms: [34]

> "The wages of men express the value of their labour in gold and from the mean value of these earnings at different ages of life, the economic value of man is calculated by taking the interest of money and the contingencies of his life into account. At the age of 25, the present value of the future earnings of an English argricultural labourer, after deducting the

cost of necessary maintenance, is £246.'

There are several legal reasons that require life to be valued; it has to be valued when cases involving claims for compensation for loss of life have to be settled, and there are requirements for compulsory insurance.   In Britain insurance is compulsory for employer's liability, motoring third party risks and nuclear accident liability. The cost of obtaining insurance cover is not a fixed factor and it depends, to some extent, on the state of the market. For example, the view has sometimes been expressed that when interest rates are high and the insurance markets are "premium hungry" insurers would cut their premiums, hoping that any losses due to claims being greater than premium income would be covered by investment income. On some occasions employer's liability risks have been accepted at a premium of 60% of the annual claims experienced over the previous 5 years.[35]

It is important to recognize that the value fixed for insurance purposes may not be the same as the total cost burden resulting from an accident.[36]   Typically factors such as production losses, retraining new staff, cleaning up the accident and investigating the accident are not covered.

Another way of judging the value of human life is to assess how much insurance cover is taken out to provide funding for any claims that might result from accidents. In 1979 insurance companies paid claims amounting to £168 million for Employer's Liability claims.[37]   In that year there were 292 fatal accidents in industry and about 9,000 other non-fatal accidents. Industry represents about 40% of all civilian employment so, of the £168 million insurance companies paid out in claims, perhaps £68 million could be attributed to industry. If the non-fatal claims average £2,000, as suggested by Bamber,[38] then the cost of fatal accidents to the insurance market averages about £170,000. The sum of £220,000 has been awarded as compensation to someone crushed in a combine harvester, so the £170,000 figure looks representative.[39] The insurance value or risk assumes the risk is known and understood. If the risk is not understood it would be virtually impossible to obtain insurance cover.

Valuing life is a useful way for assessing the order of the potential liability for compensation associated with a particular activity. A slightly different approach which is currently quite widely used is to assess the cost of saving an extra statistical life. This term is often referred to as the CSX value. One advantage of this method is that it avoids the criticism that is sometimes levelled at methods that are based on integrating lifetime earnings or lifetime production, namely that they give misleading results for the value of older people. An indication of typical CSX values is given in Table 8.[37][40]

CRITERIA FOR RANKING ECONOMIC FACTORS

Each of the analytical techniques that have just been mentioned can be used for assessing the economic significance of proposals. But the techniques, as they stand, are not directly suitable for determining the Ranking of economic factors. The optimum way of assessing the

TABLE 8   SAMPLE OF CSX VALUES

RISK	CSX £ 1982 Prices
Skyscrapers	20×10^6
General Nuclear Safety	7×10^6
Care and Road Safety Improvements	$0 - 2 \times 10^9$
Sulphur Scrubbers on Fossil Power Plants	$0.11 \times 10^6 - 5 \times 10^6$
Civil Aircraft	1.5×10^6
Reduced Infant Mortality	0.15×10^6
Diagnostic X-Ray Equipment	4×10^3

Ranking of acceptability of economic factors should give repeatable results, easily explainable results and reliabile results. These three requirements are mentioned to draw attention to the fact that the assessment technique should, with data of similar quality, give results of similar value for any proposals they are applied to. These three exacting requirements are not intended as aspersions on the efficacy of methods of economic analysis, but to expose the need for consistent, predictable and easily understandable results. If over the years the methods of analysis used do not give results that are, in general, seen to predict the outcome of proposals accurately the analysis will be discredited and decision making procedures based on them distrusted. For example the estimating procedures used for the Sydney Opera House and Concorde, both of which escalated to about ten times the original estimate, would be regarded as doubtful. [41]. Similarly the estimating procedure used for the Thames Barrier which cost about twenty times the original estimate would at best be considered doubtful. [42] Not all projects cost more than the original estimate, the fact that the later Magnox Nuclear Power Stations were built within budget shows the value of experience.

The requirement of easily understandable results is of vital importance for assessing economic factors associated with major decisions, like the acceptability of potentially hazardous plant, which are often exposed to public scrutiny and probably have to be defended openly to a lay public. This does not mean that all the supporting analysis has to be crude and simple. It merely means that the analysis has to result in a conclusion that is easily explainable and easily defensible. Accepting that the Ranking Technique provides a way of presenting the results of analysis in an understandable way the basic question is: on what should the Ranking score be based. The main possible bases for Ranking are reviewed in Table 9.

All the bases are subject to estimating errors, which as already mentioned can be massive. The significance of the emotive element that evaluating economic acceptability in terms of the cost of lives

TABLE 9   POSSIBLE BASES FOR RANKING ECONOMIC FACTORS

BASIS	COMMENT
Capital Cost	Simple straight forward. Allowance has to be made for estimating errors.
Ratio of Capital Cost to Gross National Product	Shows national significance of a project. Allowance also has to be made for estimating errors.
Return on Investment	Gives an indication of the likely commercial value of the proposal. Allowance also has to be made for estimating errors.
Cost of Lives That May be Lost	An emotive way of describing the economic risks. May not be applicable in every case. Also subject to errors.
Total Compensation	Gives a better indication of the sum at risk than simply the cost of lives that may be lost. A better solution would be to compare the net compensation, that is after allowing for the return on investment.
Opportunity Cost	Gives an indication of the value of alternatives. The problem is to identify all the relevant alternatives.
Cost/Benefit	Does draw attention to the magnitude of related gains and losses. Problem is comprehensive definition of all costs and benefits involved. Risk/benefit is considered to be just a variation of the cost/benefit genus.
Non-Dimensional Comparison of Total Cost	For comparative studies it does eliminate the emotive feature of the cost of lives, but calculation has to be carefully specified for National significance of the total cost to be determined. Also it is subject to estimating errors.

that may be lost cannot be overlooked. In the Pinto case the company involved was subject to considerable adverse publicity when it was found it had made policy decisions in terms of cost of lives that may be lost. (See page 33 and reference 20).

Net compensation seems to have some merit as it allows for all gains and losses, but is essentially just a variation of cost/benefit analysis. Opportunity cost analysis introduces another dimension, as it attempts to evaluate the comparative value of alternative forms of expenditure. The problem with opportunity cost analysis is identifying all the alternatives that should be considered. Non-dimensional comparison is most suitable for decisions inside a company or sub-parts of a major project, but not for major projects as it obscures the amount of money involved. In some cases it might be important to identify if the proposal has macro economic implications.

The question that remains is what are the most suitable criteria for assessing the acceptability Ranking of economic factors. As an indication of commercial value return on investment would be the best criteria. Simply considering the return on investment ignores the influence on national expenditure and is difficult to apply realistically to proposals related to some topics like defence or social payments. In theory opportunity cost should give the best indication of the alternatives that have to be weighed, but the method is fraught with difficulties as for any proposal the real alternatives may be hard to identify. Similar limitations apply to cost/benefit analysis. Any process of determining alternatives must, to some extent, take into account public views on priority. The issue of public views is to a large extent covered by the Ranking of socio-political factors.

This leaves non-dimensional comparison of total cost. For this method to be effective the calculation has to take into account the relationship between national expenditure or the return on investment. Also special care has to be taken to ensure that all possible alternatives are considered.

None of these comments really solves the problem of identifying a universally suitable criteria. To overcome the problem the following criterion is proposed:- The Ranking of acceptability of the economic factors should be made on the basis of the return on investment taking into account all costs and compensation that may arise during the life of the project. In Table 10 the possible relationship between these economic factors and the Ranking score are set out.

TABLE 10   POSSIBLE RELATIONSHIP BETWEEN ECONOMIC FACTORS AND
THE RANKING SCORE

ACCEPTABILITY	ECONOMIC FACTORS	SCORE RANGE	EQUIVALENT RISK ACCEPTABILITY
Unlikely to be acceptable	Overall assessment shows negative return on investment	3 - 4	1
Only acceptable if risk can be reduced	Overall assessment shows positive return on investment	2 - 3	2
Yes, subject to detailed adjustments to the proposal being made	Overall assessment shows positive return on investment could be marginal if all possible errors and uncertainty were at their most adverse value	1 - 2	3
Yes, without restriction	Overall assessment shows positive return on investment adequate after making due allowance for all possible errors and uncertainty	0 - 1	4

Chapter 7

Evaluation of Socio-political Factors for Ranking

The first step towards determining how socio-political factors can be evaluated for Ranking purposes must be to define what is included in this complex term. It is intended that socio-political factors include all the other factors that are not grouped under the heading of either technical or economic factors. The central characteristic of socio-political factors is that they are intended to reflect the whole spectrum of public opinion about the acceptability of a proposal. The spectrum of public opinion ranges from the views of individuals to political party policy views. Defined in that way shows that the socio-political factor is intended to give a balanced assessment of all aspects of public opinion related to a proposal. The Layfield report on the Sizewell 'B' Public Inquiry drew attention to the need for better communication with the public and better understanding of the public's views about the acceptability of nuclear plant.[43] Such requirements are not peculiar to nuclear plant but apply equally to any proposal that has an impact on the public whether it is operation of the Health Service, the construction of a motorway, siting an airport or siting a chemical plant.

It is recognized that socio-political terms are soft, that is they are hard to quantify. However, it is considered that the findings of public inquiries, opinion surveys, voting, consultation and epidemiological studies can give an indication of opinion. It is also appreciated that each survey method has its strengths and weakenesses, and these are discussed in more detail later in the chapter.

In the following the nature of socio-political information is first discussed, next ways it can be obtained are outlined and then several recent attempts to obtain such information are assessed. Finally criteria for assessing the significance of socio-political aspects of acceptability are given.

THE NATURE OF SOCIO-POLITICAL INFORMATION

Socio-political information essentially amounts to the measurement of public acceptability and public support for a proposal. Whether or not a proposal is regarded as acceptable requires the people making the judgement to have some understanding of the technical characteristics of the project. No honest assessment of public perception can be made unless the nature of the proposal is first explained to the public concerned in terms they understand. A proper understanding of the socio-political aspects of a proposal should enable the decision maker to make decisions about what ought to be, such decisions are quite different from technical judgements which are concerned with what can be done. Obviously, ultimately social, technical and economic judgements have to be integrated to make a soundly based comprehensive assessment of acceptability. It is a central feature of the Ranking Technique that the assessment of each group of factors is kept separate until the final comprehensive

41

assessment is made. This is necessary to prevent views about one factor contaminating views about the other factors. Furthermore the characteristic of the data are quite different, ranging from "hard" (technical data) to "soft" (socio-political data) and premature combination of these factors would not only be inappropriate, but probably very misleading.

Ideally views should be collected from the people who could or think they could be affected by the project. In practice it is not always possible to draw a simple circle around the area of interest and only deal with people inside the circle. It is often more realistic to consider all the people that have a natural concern about the project.

The difficult question that the Chernobyl accident drew attention to was the need to assess the acceptability of a potentially hazardous project to neighbouring communities not under the same government, but which could be at risk in the event of an accident. The extent to which opinions outside national boundaries have to be considered is a very sensitive political question and one which must be settled before the population whose views have to be determined can be fairly defined. A great deal of activity in this area has been initiated, under the auspices of various international organisations, directed at improving the "international" aspects of major potential hazard acceptance. Such activity is not confined to potential hazards but in most areas of business activity allowance must be made for international agreements. The agreements include agreements to accept: standards, EEC directives, insurance agreements, import quotas and restrictions on the export of sensitive defence material.

Having defined the population whose views must be identified the next question is how should their views be sought. Simply asking for a 'yes' or 'no' answer to the acceptability question is too restrictive, as it limits the amount of manoeuvre possible if a largely negative respose is first given. It is therefore better to try and build up, in an iterative way, a feeling for the shades of opinion on a proposal. This procedure could be regarded as a form of Delphi technique in which a consensus view is built up by iterative consultation. The nature of the information ultimately required can be summarized as being an assessment of the views of the people that could be affected by the proposal.

It is also necessary to recognize that the ideal situation, where the public are provided with only technically precise facts they can understand, is rarely achieved in practice. Therefore any sample tends to consist of people whose knowledge is a mixture of: technical facts, belief, and various levels of partial or mis-information propounded by interest groups. The more emotive the subject the more likely emotion is to colour views. Where there are political factors involved (such as in the Nuclear Debate) the need for an appreciation of these difficulties of understanding is important and an appropriate allowance must be made in any assessment of the views of the lay public.

HOW THE INFORMATION MAY BE OBTAINED

There are four main techniques for assessing peoples views' on acceptability. Each technique has its own special characteristics and is more suitable for some situations than others. The techniques are summarized in Table 11.

The extent to which people are willing and capable of making a considered assessment of the acceptability of a proposal depends on their knowledge of the proposal and their concern about its implications. Without an appreciation of the essential features of the proposal the public are in no position to judge its acceptability and any judgement they make would be valueless. The analyst must be careful to avoid dealing in myths and legends, whilst at the same time accepting that myths and legends colour people's views.

Whatever method of collecting the information is used six essential steps have to be taken. The six steps are shown in Fig. 4. The steps might, as explained earlier, have to be repeated until confidence is established that the population understands the problem their views are being sought on. The question still remaining of course, is "who decides that the population have understood the question?" All too often this is a synonym for they have come to the wrong conclusion. The responsibility of the analyst/decision maker is clearly highlighted here. An acceptable decision making process will be one in which both analyst and public share confidence that decisions are made properly.

RECENT SURVEYS

To illustrate the nature of the results that may be expected from surveys of opinions about controversial subjects several assessments of the popular acceptability of nuclear power are considered. The assessments are from the United Kingdom, Austria, Sweden, Switzerland and the Netherlands. A European Community Energy Opinion survey is also included.

The assessment made in the United Kingdom, to which attention is directed, is the assessment and perception of risk study made by the Psychology Department of Surrey University in 1981.[44] The study is particularly interesting because: six hazards were considered, the depths of peoples' views were assessed and the sample of people surveyed was 1189, which is fairly large. The hazards considered were:- smoking, nuclear plant, chemical, work, air pollution and the home. The depth of peoples' views were ranked as concern, worry and anxiety. Concern being the lowest level of uneasiness and anxiety being the highest level of uneasiness. The results of the survey are shown graphically in Fig. 5 and in tabular form in Table 12. For all the risks considered the degree of anxiety expressed was dramatically less than the concern expressed.

TABLE 11 TECHNIQUES FOR ASSESSING VIEWS ON ACCEPTABILITY

METHOD	STRENGTHS	LIMITATION	COMMENT
Sampling	A sample survey provides structured evidence about views on acceptability	Does not give everyone a chance to express their views about what is acceptable	The sample surveyed must be taken directly from the population affected by the decision
Voting	It is the most comprehensive way of establishing the views of a particular population	Expensive and slow to arrange. Also unless compulsion is used not every-one will vote	Provided the result of the vote is clear there should be no objection to the action taken. If the verdict is indecisive or marginal there could still be a problem
Consul-tation	Quick, provided the machinery for consultation is already established. Can give a permanent form of contact between the public and the project	Those consulted may not know the views of the whole community affected by the proposal in question. May be difficult to organize when national boundaries have to be crossed	The success of this method depends upon those consulted being fully aware of the views of the community concerned. Some forms of consultation, like a Public Inquiry can be very slow
Epidemio-logical Studies	Relates to what has already been accepted	Past experience may not be relevant	Such studies identify the likely area of concern, but they do not measure current views

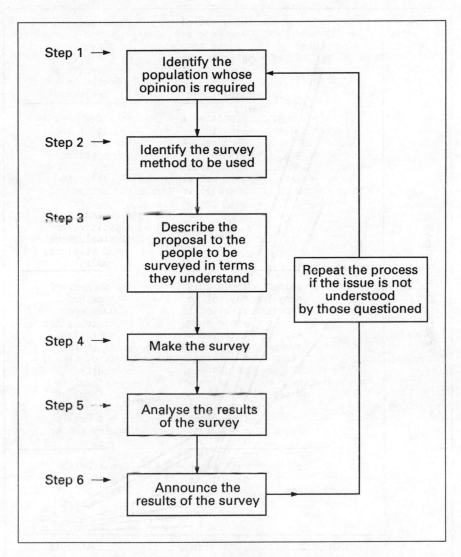

Fig 4 Steps in the opinion survey process

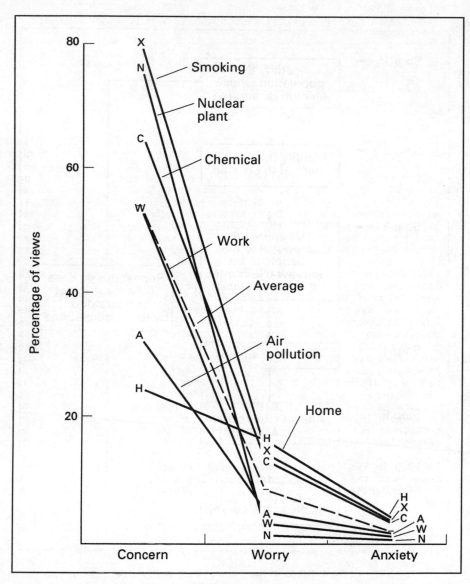

Fig 5 Percentage of sample concerned about various risks

TABLE 12   CONCERN ABOUT SIX HAZARDS

Level of Uneasiness Expressed	Smoking	Nuclear Plant	Chemical	Work	Air Pollution	Home	Average
Concern	80%	76%	64%	53%	32%	24%	54.8%
Worry	14%	1%	13%	3%	4%	16%	8.5%
Anxiety	3%	0.4%	3%	0.7%	1%	4%	2%

It will be seen that the greatest concern was about smoking for which 80% expressed concern, the least concern was for the familiar hazards in the home about which only 24% expressed concern. The average level of concern over the six hazards was 54.6%, with nuclear plant being the second highest at 76%. The average worry about the hazards was 8%, with nuclear only 1% of those surveyed. Anxiety was even lower with an average level of 2% and anxiety about nuclear being the lowest at 0.4%. It must be remembered that these were pre-Chernobyl views. In any case views change with time and the nature of such changes are illustrated later by the results from the European Community Survey.

The Austrian Survey was made as part of the Joint IAEA/IIASA Risk Assessment Project of the Acceptability of five energy sources, namely nuclear, coal, oil, hydro and solar.[45] This survey is interesting as it was made shortly before the referendum in 1978 in which the Austrian electorate decided against nuclear power. The survey was made by means of a questionnaire. Two hundred and twenty four members of the Austrian public took part in the survey; the sample being stratified by age, education, sex and geographical location (Vienna, provincial capital and rural).[46] Attributes were assessed using a semantic differential technique on a series of seven point scales. The members of the public who participated in the survey were most favourable towards the renewable sources, hydro and solar energy and as a whole least favourable towards nuclear energy. The survey can be considered as giving a clear indication of the likely outcome of the referendum.

In 1979 in Sweden a referendum about the acceptability of nuclear power was seen as a way of solving a very serious political conflict that had developed.[47] The referendum was held in March 1980. The options for voters were:-

1) Shut down the six operating reactors within ten years and plan for six additional reactors to be abandoned.
2) Twelve nuclear power stations to be used as long as necessary to meet the demand for electricity.
3) Was as option 2 but in addition called for the "socialisation" of the production and distribution of electricity. In other words it called for state control over nuclear power. It also included the setting up of local safety committees at each nuclear power plant.
4) Return a blank vote which was intended to signify nuclear policy

should be resolved by Parliament.
5)   There was the unofficial option of abstaining from voting.

75.7% of the eligible population voted, of these 58% voted for the yes options (option 2 and 3) and 38% voted for the no option (option 1). In the year prior to the voting date there had been a campaign to educate the population about the problems of nuclear power. As 50% of men and 60% of women believed that they were inadequately informed and 58% voted for the yes option the anti-nuclear campaign does not appear to have been particularly successful. After Chernobyl the proposed planned closures were reappraised by an expert group that recommended a planned phase out of nuclear power between 1987 and 2005 with the intervening time being used to develop alternative sources of electricity supply.

It has been suggested that there are eight groups in Swedish society with specific attitudes towards nuclear power and that their views were in close agreement with the results of the referendum and public opinion polls.[45] Examination of these groups suggests that attitudes to nuclear power are to some extent dependent on, or conditioned by, a deeper social-psychological attitude which may not be easily modified. The view has been expressed that the proportion of the groups will only change slowly with changes in the social economy and the social structure, and that they are unlikely to be influenced in the short term by action directed specifically to encourage acceptance of nuclear power.[45] It has also been suggested that the present shift away from employment in the manufacturing industry towards increasing employment in the services and social sectors may harden the opposition to nuclear power.[45]

In Switzerland there have been two major votes (known in Switzerland as initiatives) to establish the strength of the opposition to nuclear power.[46] In February 1979 there was a vote to limit nuclear reactor operating licenses to 25 years and to place unlimited responsibility on owners for all damage up to 90 years. The proposal was rejected by 51.7% to 48.3%, but only 49% of the electorate voted. In May 1979 there was a referendum on a revision of the Swiss Atomic Energy Act. The revision was supported by 68.9% of those voting. The proportion of the electorate voting was down to 37%, which is not surprising as the referendum was the second in three months.

An analysis by the Research Centre for Swiss Politics of the University of Bern identified the most important considerations in determining the votes as being: 45% of those against nuclear power agreed with the statement that nuclear power stations were dangerous, while 40% of those in favour of nuclear power accepted that it was necessary to alleviate the energy shortage.[46] The main area of public concern was considered to be the question of the safe disposal of radioactive waste.[46]

The Swiss Atomic Energy Association (ASPEA), the Union of Swiss Power Stations (UCS) and the National Cooperative Society for the Storage of Radioactive Waste (NAGRA) have each tried to educate the Swiss public about the real nature of risks associated with nuclear power.[47] The education process has included distribtution of information, sponsoring conferences and visits to power stations.

In 1982 a survey was made for the acceptability of the industrial risks in the Rijnmond area of the Netherlands.[48]   Although not specifically concerned with nuclear power the technique developed is relevant.   The survey was made by interviewing a stratified sample of 600 people.   370 of these people lived in the Rijnmond district within 4km of the risk area, 73 lived further away in the centre of Rotterdam and 70 lived at Apeldoorn in a rural part of the Netherlands.   About 15% of those approached refused to be interviewed.   For this survey a form of questioning called a SITE model (Sense of Insecurity with Respect to Threat from the Physical Environment) was developed.   The aim of the questions being to determine to what extent the public feel threatened by their technological and industrial environment, the extent to which they can cope with their feeling of insecurity and whether a specific technological threat represents a daily problem. The questionnaires used took several forms, with the most extensive questionnaire being presented to those living closest to the risk and the shortest version being presented to those living furthest away, namely the control-group in Apeldoorn.

The important conclusions from the survey are that the SITE model gave a reliable way of assessing public concern about industrial hazards and the public are as much concerned with understanding the issues of control and management of risks as understanding the intricacies of hazard assessment.

The survey that the Commission of the European Communities had made of the public's perception of the energy situation and their attitude to various sources of energy, particularly nuclear power, brings the whole question of acceptability into focus.[49]   The survey was made in October 1984 and consisted of putting twenty identical questions to nationally representative samples of the population aged fifteen and over, a total of 9,911 people being involved.   Each person was interviewed at home by a professional interviewer.   Somewhat similar surveys had been performed in 1978 and 1982.   The 1982 results provide a base to compare the 1984 results with and give an indication of how views change.   The changes in views within countries being greatest.

The survey looked at nuclear power from three main angles which were:

1)   The basic option for or against the development of nuclear power stations.
2)   The credibility of the economic arguments.
3)   The risks of nuclear power stations.

The important findings of this survey are summarized in Tables 13, 14, 15 and 16.   Table 13 shows views on the advantages of developing nuclear power stations.   These results suggest that the greatest support for the development of nuclear power comes from those with the highest level of education and the greatest satisfaction with democracy.   The results also showed that nuclear power tended to be supported by those with a preference for: independence, less pollution and priority for energy policies.

TABLE 13   VIEWS ON THE ADVANTAGES OF DEVELOPING NUCLEAR POWER

COUNTRY	WORTHWHILE	NO PARTICULAR ADVANTAGE	UNACCEPTABLE RISKS	DO NOT KNOW
Belgium	37	8	45	10
Denmark	22	10	48	20
Germany	45	8	30	17
Greece	17	3	70	10
France	55	4	30	11
Ireland	13	14	62	11
Italy	41	6	43	10
Luxembourg	28	18	46	8
Netherlands	37	7	47	9
United Kingdom	41	13	37	9
LEVEL OF EDUCATION				
Low	37	9	38	16
Average	48	8	35	9
High	51	5	38	6
SATISFACTION WITH DEMOCRACY				
Very Satisfied	56	9	25	10

The results in Table 14 show that in 1982 and 1984 a chemical plant was considered more hazardous than a nuclear power station. In 1982 a nuclear power plant was considered less hazardous than an explosives factory, but in 1984 nuclear power plants and explosives factories were considered to be equal risks.

Table 15 shows in more detail how concern about nuclear power risks appears to have increased from 1982 to 1984, particularly with regard to concern about the risk of explosions and the storage of radioactive waste.

TABLE 14   ANALYSIS OF ANSWERS IN 1982 AND 1984 TO THE QUESTION: WHICH THREE INSTALLATIONS IN YOUR OPINION, CREATE THE GREATEST RISKS FOR PEOPLE LIVING NEARBY.

	PERCENTAGE CONSIDERED MOST IMPORTANT RISK	
INSTALLATION	1982	1984
Oil Refinery	23	26
Coal-Fired Power Stations	2	10
Large Airfield or Airport	16	13
Food Processing Factory	2	1
Nuclear Power Station	60	64
Chemical Plant (Producing sulphuric acid, ammonia, chlorine, etc.)	71	80
Explosives Factory	64	64
Natural Gas Processing Plant	15	11
Furniture Factory	1	1
Dam Producing Hydro-Electric Power	6	6
Don't Know	5	3

TABLE 15   SUMMARY OF CHANGES BETWEEN 1982 AND 1984 IN VIEWS ON NUCLEAR RISKS

HAZARDS MOST CONCERN ABOUT	1982	1984
Power station explosion	23	35
Radioactive emissions whilst the power station is operating	51	56
Dangers of storing radioactive waste	57	69
None of these		4
Don't know	13	4

Table 16 shows the views in some countries have changed more than in others. The average view of all the countries has changed little. It has been suggested that there has been a decline in the credibility of the economic arguments for building more nuclear power stations.[48]

The general conclusions that seem to be justified are:- 1) That a survey on the scale of the EEC survey shows the differences in views between social groups and countries and the magnitude of the changes that can take place in two years. 2) Although the survey mentioned did not cover every country the spread of data presented gives a clear indication of the variation of views that may be expected in a relatively small geographical area. By analogy in a large country like the United States of America it is expected that there would be similar variations of view across the country. 3) Taken together the survey results show that socio-political factors related to complex decisions can be measured by carefully designed surveys. For an effective survey to be made the nature of the risk must be explained to the population being surveyed. But it has to be recognized that opinions can change quite quickly. 4) A survey does not represent any kind of commitment by the people being surveyed, whereas voting procedures may be binding. 5) There appears to be some merit in involving people in the area of the project, with the management of the risk. This involvement may be through some form of local liaison committee. Such committees can also help develop mutual confidence.

CRITERIA FOR RANKING THE SOCIO-POLITICAL FACTOR

When a proposal involves a decision about the acceptability of the scheme either to the public in general or a particular section of the public, the opinion of the relevant public must be assessed in quantitative terms. Although voting is the ideal way of making such a quantitative assessment it is accepted that a properly designed survey can give a sound assessment of opinion. The criteria for determining the Ranking justified for socio-political factors is simply that: the acceptability of a proposal in socio-political terms should be assessed quantitatively and the quantitative evidence used as the basis for Ranking. In Table 17 a possible relationship between socio-political factors and the Ranking score are set out. The efficacy of this criteria and the other criteria proposed are discussed in Chapter 9.

TABLE 16   SHIFT OF OPINIONS ABOUT NUCLEAR POWER BETWEEN
           1982 AND 1984

	COUNTRY										
ADVANTAGES OF DEVELOPING NUCLEAR POWER	B*	DK*	D*	EL*	F*	IRL*	I*	L*	NL*	UK*	EC*
Worthwhile	+10	-3	+8	+2	+4	0	+7	-4	+3	+2	+5
No Particular Advantage	-1	+1	-5	-3	0	-7	+1	+10	+1	-4	-3
Unacceptable Risks	+8	-1	+3	+20	-1	+15	+4	-3	-1	0	+1
NUCLEAR POWER STATIONS AVOID THE NEED TO CUT ELECTRICITY CONSUMPTION											
True	+6	-15	-8	+7	-6	+3	-1	-16	-7	0	-3
Not True	+11	+14	+16	+4	+9	¹15	+8	+22	+11	+5	+10
SERIOUSNESS OF A CUT DUE TO REJECTION OF NUCLEAR ENERGY											
Very Serious	-7	-19	-6	+5	0	+5	-1	-4	-3	-5	-3
Not Very Serious	+17	+12	+11	+3	0	+1	+3	+8	+3	¹7	+7
HAZARDOUS INSTALLATIONS											
Nuclear Power Cited	+7	0	+6	+10	-4	-11	+2	-1	-2	+10	+4
HAZARDS OF NUCLEAR POWER STATIONS											
Radioactive waste	+12	-4	+5	+10	-3	+21	+2	0	+9	+11	+5
Storage of waste	+22	+9	+16	+9	+3	+22	+13	+2	+13	+10	+12

```
* B   = Belgium          I  = Italy
  DK  = Denmark          L  = Luxembourg
  D   = West Germany     NL = Netherlands
  EL  = Spain            UK = United Kingdom
  F   = France           EC = Whole European Community
  IRL = Ireland
```

<u>TABLE 17</u>   POSSIBLE RELATIONSHIP BETWEEN SOCIO-POLITICAL
FACTORS AND THE RANKING SCORE

ACCEPTABILITY	SOCIO-POLITICAL FACTORS	SCORE RANGE	EQUIVALENT RISK ACCEPTABILITY RANK
Unlikely to be acceptable	Less than 1/3rd of the population judged to be in favour of the proposal	3 - 4	1
Only acceptable if risk can be reduced	Between 1/3rd and 1/2 of the relevant population judged to be in favour of the proposal	2 - 3	2
Yes, subject to detailed adjustments to the proposal being made	Between 1/2 and 2/3rds of the relevant population judged to be in favour of the proposal	1 - 2	3
Yes without restriction	Over 2/3rds of the relevant population judged to be in favour of the proposal	0 - 1	4

Chapter 8
Assessment of the Potential Efficacy of the Ranking Technique

During the early development of the Ranking Technique it was tested on several different types of proposition. In the following, five of these tests are examined to provide a basis for assessing the efficacy and adaptability of the Technique. Four of the tests concerned proposals that had generated a certain amount of controversy. These four are: the Canvey Island Development, the Moss Morran pipeline, the Rijnmond liquified natural gas terminal and the Channel Tunnel. The fifth test was an assessment of the public safety implications of energy options and was of a slightly different nature.

It is important to note that these 'tests' of the Ranking Technique were all of a 'post hoc' nature. It is accepted that there are differences between this use of the method, and cases where it is used during the primary decision making process we return to the question of the guidelines for practical applications in Chapter 10.

The Canvey Island project involved a proposal to build an oil refinery with a capacity of four million tonnes/year on Canvey Island, which is located on the North Shore of the Thames twenty seven miles east of London. Canvey Island measures approximately nine miles by two and a half miles. About 33,000 people live in the area. In the area there are tank storage installations for: Texaco Ltd. and London and Coastal Oil Wharves Ltd., also the British Gas Corporation have a methane terminal there. Close to Canvey Island and in the general area covered by the proposed development Shell UK Oil and the Mobil Oil Company have large oil refineries, also Calor Gas Ltd., have a plant for filling cylinders with liquified petroleum gases.

As a result of a Public Inquiry into the desirability of revoking the planning permission that had been granted the Government asked the Health and Safety Commission to make an assessment of the acceptability of the risks associated with existing installations and the cost of the assessment was £400,000.[50] Three years after the first Canvey Island study report the results of a second more detailed study of the issue were published.[51] It is on the basis of the information published in these two reports that the Ranking of the acceptability of Canvey was tested.

The Moss Morran project was for a liquefied energy gas terminal and pipeline, which was planned as part of the facilities required to exploit the Brent oil and gas field in the North Sea. More exactly the proposal was that the oil and gas should be brought ashore by pipeline at St. Fergus and then after some processing transmitted via the Cruden Bay area to Moss Morran for processing into fuel and feedstocks such as propane, butane and ethylene. From the processing plant the feedstocks would be transported, mainly by sea, to their ultimate destination. Because the decision about acceptability of the project was considered to be of national importance the government called for the decision to be made centrally rather than at local government level.[52]

The process of assessing the acceptability of the proposal involved a public inquiry, a special report by a firm of consultants, advice by the Health and Safety Executive and discussion with local authorities. Concern about the potential hazard was particularly involved with the possibility of a cloud of hydrocarbon vapour escaping and being ignited by the radio-frequency transmissions in the St. Fergus area. The Health and Safety Executive published two reports on the technical assessment of the hazards involved and it is on the basis of the information given in those reports that the Ranking of risk acceptability was tested.[53][54] The technical assessment figures used are those given in the Health and Safety Executive's reappraisal reference 54.

The history of the Rijnmond Case is complicated and has its origins in the early 1970's when plans were made to import large quantitites of liquified natural gas (LNG) from Algeria.[55] The two main contenders for the site were Rotterdam and Eemshaven. The decision involved the Dutch cabinet, several government departments, the local government authorities of the areas concerned and public meetings. Safety implications and public perception of the acceptability of risk were important factors in deciding which site should be selected. The case is particularly interesting for the fact that local politics appear to have been a more important influence on the final decision than marginal differences in the quantified estimates of the risks involved.[55]

Discussion of a fixed link across the Channel has been going on for nearly 200 years.[56] Following the Anglo-French summit meeting in London in September 1981 an expert study group was established to evaluate the technical and economic arguments for a fixed Channel link.[57] The group advised that they considered the balance of advantage lay with bored twin rail tunnels with a vehicle shuttle.[57] Discussions about the acceptability of the various proposals came to something of a climax at the end of 1985 when the Transport Secretary, Nicholas Ridley, announced that he was then of the opinion that work on the project must start within two years.[57] Ten schemes were submitted but attention was concentrated on four main proposals. Consultants were employed to analyse the schemes and their reports were presented to the Department of Transport in December 1985. Nicholas Ridley announced that instead of a public inquiry there would be extensive public consultation,[58] the public consultation being based on 15-page summaries of the proposals. The test of the Ranking Technique is based on the evidence contained in the 15-page summaries, so the test was made on the same basis that the general public could have used.[57] In fact the Ranking test was made before the British and French Governments announced, in Lille on the 20th January 1986, that they had accepted the rail tunnel proposal. However, in the discussion of the efficacy of the Ranking Technique the implications of the decision and the subsequent reaction are discussed.

The test of the Technique on the assessment of the public safety implications of energy options had a rather different emphasis. It was not concerned with a specific project but with assessing the

policy significance of the public safety implications of the likely
future options for energy supply. The options considered were fossil,
fuel, nuclear power and hydroelectric power. It was recognized that
with the length of time it takes to build a power station the pattern
of power generating stations will only change slowly. It was also
recognized that there are enormous variations from country to country
in the sources of power used, for example in Norway hydroelectric
power is of major importance and in France nuclear power is the main
source of electrical power production.

CANVEY ISLAND

An attempt to Rank the acceptability of the Canvey Island proposal was
described in reference 2. Two official studies were made of the
risks inherent in the proposal and the results reported in references
50 and 51. From the first study it was concluded that the risks
associated with the various industrial installations would be reduced
if certain modifications were made. The conclusion was also drawn
that provided certain design and operational conditions were
satisfied, there would be no health or safety objection to the
construction of the proposed new refineries. The main objective of
the second report, which was published three years after the first,
was to show the result of making the modifications identified in the
first report show the result of improvements in the data and
improvements in the risk assessment methodology. The first report
showed the annual risk of death to an individual in the area covered
by the study was 7.40×10^{-4} per year. In the second report it was
shown that the average risk figure had been reduced to 0.35×10^{-4} per
year.

The information from the studies has been interpreted for Ranking
purposes in the following way:-

At the time of the first report the acceptability of the level of risk
associated with the area was doubtful. The technical risks were not
acceptable as the regulatory body required modifications to be made.
The economic aspects of the risks were judged to be acceptable as the
owners of the various installations involved were willing to modify
them and to continue to operate them. Concern about the socio-
political aspects was high, as it was considered necessary to hold a
public inquiry and to commission detailed studies of the significance
of the risks.

By the time the second report was issued, the significance of the
various factors related to acceptability of risk had changed
considerably. The work done in the three years following publication
of the first report allowed estimates of the technical significance of
the risks to be reduced making them more acceptable. The economics of
the plants must have become slightly more favourable as the threat of
closure was removed.

The Ranking based on the two reports is summarized in Table 18.
Although the evidence was rather vague, particularly with respect to
the technical and socio-political aspects, it does show how the
Ranking Technique can give a logical structure to the analysis of

acceptability. Also the example shows how the Ranking of acceptability can be refined as better data becomes available.

TABLE 18　RANKING OF CANVEY ISLAND RISKS

BASIS	SCORES OF SUB-FACTORS			RANK
	TECHNICAL	ECONOMIC	SOCIO-POLITICAL	
FIRST REPORT[50]	2 1/2	1	1 1/2	2
SECOND REPORT[51]	1	1	1	3

MOSS MORRAN

In addition to the technical assessments, mentioned earlier, that were made the directors of planning of the three local authorities concerned jointly prepared a report on the socio-economic impact of the proposal. The deliberations about the possibility of a hydrocarbon vapour cloud forming and being ignited (possibly by radio frequency emissions) added two years to the decision process. It was finally shown on the basis of the tests at the Shell Research Centre, Bradford University, and on site that radio-frequency transmissions were unlikely to produce sufficient power to reach the minimum required for ignition.[53][54]

The risks were assessed, by the Health and Safety Executive, as being in the range of 1 to 4×10^{-6} per year of there being a leak from the pipeline that would put people in the area of risk.[54] The report concluded that such a level of risk, "would not be such as to lead to a recommendation that a Construction Authorisation should be withheld on health and safety grounds". Attention is drawn to the fact that although a quantitative consequence analysis had been made of the probability of various types of failure were expressed in qualitative terms like low, very low or extremely low and no estimate of the possibility of multiple fatalities was given.[53][54]

There has been some criticism of the adequacy of the risk analysis both in respect of accuracy and thoroughness.[59] Something of the official concern about the safety and risk justification of the Moss Morran site appears to be reflected in conditions that were attached to the outline planning permissions granted to Shell and Esso.[60] Forty eight conditions were attached to both permissions.[60] The most important condition from the safety point of view being the requirement that a full hazard operability audit should be made before the facilities would be allowed to be commissioned. The importance attached to the audit is indicated by the fact that the Secretary of State decided the audit must be to his satisfaction and not just to the satisfaction of the Health and Safety Executive.[60]

The Ranking considered to be justified is described in Table 19. With the benefit of hindsight the Moss Morran proposal appears to justify acceptable Ranking as a subject to certain action. The assumption being that the process of making a full hazard and operability audit would result in the introduction of any alterations required to make the proposal acceptable.

TABLE 19   RANKING JUSTIFIED FOR THE MOSS MORRAN PROPOSAL

FACTOR	RANKING SCORE	JUSTIFICATION
TECHNICAL	2	All the advice, which was a mixture of qualitative and quantitative assessments suggested the propsals were acceptable subject to detailed justification. The installations are similar to those accepted in other parts of the world.
ECONOMIC	1	National Energy Policy required the Brent oil and gas field to be exploited. The financial risks of the operation were undertaken by private companies and were consistent with the scale of risk they undertook in other parts of their work.
SOCIO-POLITICAL	1	The proposals were accepted at Government level but the Secretary of State made it a condition that he must be satisfied with the safety audit. The opposition to the proposals was essentially of a limited local nature.
TOTAL RANKING SCORE	4	SO A RISK RANK 3 IS JUSTIFIED

RIJNMOND

Discussion about which was the most acceptable site has been divided into three rounds. Round 'A' was the period up to the final signing of the contract for the supply of LNG and included the preliminary search for a terminal site. Round 'B' involved the cabinet, several government departments and at this stage it was recognized that siting of an LNG terminal involved several issues such as: energy policy, the environment, safety, land use and regional planning. At the beginning of this round Rotterdam was the preferred site and discussions were held with the local authorities in the region. These included the Province of Zuid-Holland, Rijnmond Public Authority, and the City of Rotterdam. These discussions showed that the authorities, particularly the Rijnmond Public Authority were likely to apply stringent safety requirements to any LNG terminal. The involvement of the Rijnmond Public Authority is the reason the decision became known

as the 'Rijnmond Decision'. In simple terms it was considered that
discussion of these requirements was likely to delay the start of
delivering LNG and this led to Eemshaven being reconsidered as the
site for the terminal. Round 'C' was the final round which ended with
the cabinet deciding in favour of Eemshaven.

In April 1978 the Rotterdam and Groningen local authorities were each
given three months in which to formulate their views on the
acceptability of an LNG terminal in their area. During this period
there were formal council debates and public meetings at which the
public and interest groups could express their views. The views of
the local authorities were presented to the cabinet in June 1978. In
August 1978 the cabinet announced its preference for Eemshaven
primarily on socio-economic regional industrial grounds. The decision
was debated at considerable length in Parliament and finally approved
in October 1978.

The view has been expressed that in part the reason that the decision
went in favour of Eemshaven was that the Governor of Groningen was a
skillful politician and a long standing member of one of the parties
in power.[55]   In this context the final decision appears to have been
guided more by political opportunity than by consistent government
policies, strategies or decision procedures. This in many ways
underlines the significance of the socio-political factors in any
assessment of acceptability. Attention must also be drawn to the fact
that the decision was in conflict with the official advice of the
Interdepartmental Coordinating Committee for North Sea Affairs
(ICONA).[55]   The official ICONA report can be criticised because it
intentionally did not consider either local risk perception in
relation to public and official acceptance of LNG or the political
importance attached by some interested parties to the siting of the
terminal. These two factors seem to have had a dominant influence on
the decision.[55]

Although ICONA can be criticised for not considering local opinion it
was the only coordinating body that included representatives of all
the relevant ministries and in preparing its advice it took account of
all aspects of national policy.[62]   ICONA advised that from their
evaluation of economics, energy policy and environmental impact they
preferred the Maasvlakte site near the Hook von Holland for the LNG
terminal. The ICONA view on the risks associated with the Maasvlakte
and Eemshaven sites was the risks with both sites were approximately
equal.[62]

In addition to the local authorities, the trade unions were in favour
of Eemshaven.[62]   The Environmentalist Groups, Shipowners Association
and Electricity Corporation were against Eemshaven.[62]   The
Shipowners saw some navigation and operational problems and some risks
could be associated with Eemshaven. The Electricity Corporation saw
some risk to their existing coal-fired power station. A comparison of
the official quantitative risk data is given in Table 20.[63]

On the basis of the evidence available it was possible to Rank the
Maasvlakte and Eemshaven sites in a similar way to the way the Moss
Morran proposal was Ranked. The justification of the Ranking of the

TABLE 20   COMPARISON OF THE OFFICIAL MAASVLAKTE AND
EEMSHAVEN RISK DATA

RISK	MAASVLAKTE	EEMSHAVEN
Probability of a major accident. (If other additional safety measures were adopted).	3×10^{-7} (3×10^{-8})	10^{-7} (5×10^{-8})
Maximum consequences Number of deaths Number of casualties	$0.5 - 2 \times 10^{4}$ $1 - 4 \times 10^{4}$	$0.5 - 2 \times 10^{3}$ $1 - 4 \times 10^{3}$
Material third party damage (Dutch Guilders)	18×10^{9}	not given
Increase in risk of individual death	3×10^{-6}	$<3 \times 10^{-7}$

Maasvlakte site is given in Table 21 and the Ranking of the Eemshaven
site is given in Table 22

The Ranking of the comprehensive risk assessment of the Maasvlakte and
Eemshaven options shows the significance of the various factors. It
was perhaps a combination of a marginal technical advantage with a
marginal socio-political advantage that made the decision makers
decide in favour of Eemshaven. It is unlikely that the slight
advantages given by either technical or socio-political factors would
have been sufficient to swing the decision in favour of Eemshaven.

TABLE 21   RANKING JUSTIFIED FOR THE MAASVLAKTE SITE

FACTOR	SCORE	JUSTIFICATION
TECHNICAL	2	Probability of a major accident put at 3×10^{-8} and the increase in risk of individual death 3×10^{-6}. The slightly high score given because some engineering work required.
ECONOMIC	1	The economic need for an LNG terminal was agreed. Maasvlakte is slightly nearer to the point of use for LNG. The third party risk is acceptable.
SOCIO-POLITICAL	1	Although the site was rejected by the cabinet and the parliament, the socio-political arguments were marginal.
TOTAL SCORE	4	SO RISK RANK 3 IS JUSTIFIED

TABLE 22   RANKING JUSTIFIED FOR THE EEMSHAVEN SITE

FACTOR	SCORE	JUSTIFICATION
TECHNICAL	1	Probability of a major accident put at 5×10^{-8} and the increase of risk of individual death $<3 \times 10^{-7}$. The risk of individual death is lower than Maasvlakte so that is why a lower ranking score is considered to be justified.
ECONOMIC	1	The economic need for an LNG terminal was agreed. Economic benefit of development to the area accepted. Economic acceptability of risks the same as for Maasvlakte.
SOCIO-POLITICAL	0	The site was accepted. There was political support for the site and there was Trade Union support for the site.
TOTAL SCORE	2	SO RISK RANK 4 IS JUSTIFIED

CHANNEL TUNNEL

The four Channel Crossing proposals considered were: the Eurobridge, the Euroroute, the Channel Tunnel and the Channel Expressway. The main technical factors of the proposals are summarized in Table 23 the economic factors are summarized in Table 24 and the socio-political factors in Table 25.

The evidence that was used was that given in the Official Case presented to the British Parliament.[64] There was no attempt in the reference 64 to quantify the magnitude or the probability of the technical risks involved. In the evidence presented attention was not drawn to such facts as: the real experience with the material proposed for the suspension-bridge cables was only about one seventh of the life proposed with the material and no justification was given for the acceptability of the explosion risk in such a long tunnel. On the evidence available the Ranking of the four proposals was built up together with the option of not constructing a fixed crossing. The justification for the scoring of each factor is shown in Tables 26, 27 and 28. Evaluation of the economic implications of the proposals showed that the total cost of the proposals was likely to be a significant factor in the economies of the two countries. Possible variation in total cost is a factor that has to be considered, as experience has shown that the cost of a major novel project often far exceeds initial estimates. For example quite unrelated projects like the Sydney Opera House and Concorde escalated to about ten times the original estimate.[41] The Thames barrier was originally estimated to cost £23 million and actually cost £461 million.[65]

TABLE 23 SUMMARY OF MAIN CHANNEL CROSSING TECHNICAL FACTORS OF INTEREST

PROPOSAL	TECHNICAL FACTORS	
	CONSTRUCTION FEATURES	HAZARD CONCERNS
EUROBRIDGE (64)	Suspension bridge of seven 5 km spans plus 6m diameter rail tunnel. Traffic lanes enclosed in a Superferrolo tube. The suspension cables 1.4m dia Parafil.	Suspension tower to with-stand impact of a 250,000 ton ship. Oscillation of spans. Ventilation of traffic tube. Explosions on the bridge. Driver fatigue. Life of components.
EUROROUTE (64)	For road transport two bridges from each coast to artificial islands. Islands linked by tunnel on the sea bed. Also a rail tunnel on sea bed coast to coast.	Ventilation of the tunnels. Earth movement. Resistance of the 34 protective caissons to damage by shipping. Explosions in the tunnel. Life of components.
CHANNEL TUNNEL (64)	A 3-tunnel system, two railway and one service tunnels. Terminals for loading and unloading road vehicles on and off trains.	Ventilation. Earth movements. Life of components. Explosions in the tunnels.
CHANNEL EXPRESSWAY (64)	A twin tunnel system, each tunnel taking both road and rail traffic. Would be the largest drive through the tunnel in the world.	Ventilation. Earth movement. Life of components. Driver fatigue.

In assessing the socio-political factors only some objection by people living in the area of the terminals was reported in the discussion in Parliament and the Press. This is not surprising as no carefully designed survey of public opinion was made. The only surveys made were by local papers and are considered to be of questionable value. [66]

The overall Ranking of acceptability is shown in Table 29. The conclusion that appears to be justified from the overall Ranking is that the Channel Tunnel Proposal is the most acceptable and the no fixed link option the least acceptable. Also the Channel Tunnel Proposal was shown to be subject to the least number of technical reservations.

Ultimately the Government reached its decision by evaluating the qualitative advice of a multi-disciplinary assessment team. The

TABLE 24   SUMMARY OF MAIN CHANNEL CROSSING ECONOMIC
FACTORS OF INTEREST

PROPOSAL	PROPOSING GROUP	ESTIMATED COST	COMPLETION TIME	SUGGESTED TOLL	RETURN
EURO-BRIDGE	Laing, Brown & Root ICI	£5.9 bn	5 years	Comparable to sea ferries	21-22% Pay back 6 - 11 years
EURO-ROUTE	Trafalgar House, British Steel and Banks.	Motorway link £7.2 bn Rail link £3.5 bn	5 years for bridge 8 years for tunnel	Comparable to sea ferries	17% gross Complete pay back 15 years
CHANNEL TUNNEL	5 UK & 2 French construction companies and 3 French banks.	Max. debt £4.75 bn allowing £1bn for contingen-cies.	7 years from Government announcing decision	10% below existing ferry tariffs	19% rate of return. Complete pay back 15 years
CHANNEL EXPRESS WAY	British Ferries Ltd.	£2.5bn including construction period interest	5 years	Cars 50% cheaper & lorries the same as ferries	Return on equity 27%

published data gave the impression that there had been no consistent attempt to quantify the significance of the risks and uncertainties inherent in the proposals. Assessing which proposal is the most acceptable on relatively thin data is not an unusual position for a decision maker in the pre-contract stage. It would be easy to say the adequacy of the Ranking was limited by the adequacy of the data available in reference 64, but such a trite comment would be misleading and would understate the significance of the issue. It is assumed that evidence is honest, the facts relevant and the proposals constructed by people with appropriate specialist knowledge. It is appreciated that a different conclusion might have been reached if there had been access to all the official data. The assessment was made in a consistent way and the Ranking scores allocated reflect an unbiased assessment of the acceptability of the main features of the proposals. Even though comprehensive quantified data was not available the structured form of the Ranking Technique allowed a logically defensible comparative assessment of acceptability to be made. It is also clear that the quality of the Ranking would be improved with better data.

ENERGY OPTIONS

The assessment of the public safety risk implications of energy options was aimed at determining if there was any significant

TABLE 25   SUMMARY OF CHANNEL CROSSING SOCIO-POLITICAL FACTORS

PROPOSAL	PUBLIC CONSULTATION	ADVANTAGES FOR PUBLIC	DISADVANTAGES FOR PUBLIC	ARGUMENT FOR	ARGUMENT AGAINST
EURO-BRIDGE	No public inquiry. Questions may be raised in parliament. Simple poll showed 63% in favour of fixed link.	Reduces journey time. Greater efficiency should improve employment.	Economic adjustment in Dover and Calais areas. Loss of agricultrual land for terminals.	Improve European employment.	High cost technology uncertain
EURO-ROUTE	As Eurobridge above.	As Eurobridge above.	As Eurobridge above.	As Eurobridge above.	High cost, driver safety and ventilation.
CHANNEL TUNNEL	As Eurobridge above.	As Eurobridge above.	As Eurobridge above.	Less risk of accident.	Road to rail change.
CHANNEL EXPRESS WAY	As Eurobridge above.	Also has benefit of both road and rail.	As Eurobridge above.	As Euro-bridge above.	Driver safety & ventilation.

difference in the options available that should influence future energy policy. It was assumed the world pattern of energy consumption will continue with crude petroleum taking first place and coal and lignites in second place. Third and fourth place being taken by natural gas and nuclear energy. But the precise proportions may change, it seems likely that there will be some fall in coal consumption. The long term trend in oil consumption is rather more difficult to predict after the recent price changes. The contribution of nuclear power will probably gradually increase, but it has to be recognized that as a result of Chernobyl many countries are considering the shape of their nuclear programmes.

Similarly the world pattern of electrical power production is only likely to change slowly with conventional power stations still holding pride of place for some years yet. Conventional power stations being defined as coal, oil and gas fuelled stations. Hydroelectric stations, defined very liberally to include pumped storage and tidal power, coming second but being more closely challenged by nuclear power. Of course there are enormous variations from country to country in the pattern of power stations. For example: in Norway hydroelectric power is of major importance and in France nuclear power is the main source of electrical power production. Some countries are entirely without hydroelectric power and some without nuclear power.

TABLE 26   CHANNEL CROSSING TECHNICAL FACTOR RANK SCORE
            OF PROPOSALS

PROPOSAL	TECHNICAL FACTOR CONCERNS	SCORE JUSTIFIED
EURO-BRIDGE	Limited data about life of Superferrolo and Parafil. No information about: oscillation of bridge, earth movements, adequacy of ventilation, driver fatigue, water tightness and resistance to explosions.	Considerable technical justification of new materials required. Proposed score 2.
EURO-ROUTE	Resistance to earth movements, ventilation, driver fatigue, bridge oscillation, tunnel water tightness and resistance to explosions.	Considerable technical justification of design required. Proposed score 2.
CHANNEL TUNNEL	Earth movements, ventilation, water tightness, resistance to explosions and driver fatigue.	Some justification of design required. Proposed score 2.
CHANNEL EXPRESS WAY	Will tunnel be disturbed by earth movements, adequacy of ventilaton, water tightness, resistance to explosions and driver fatigue.	Some justification of design required. Proposed score 2.
NO FIXED LINK CROSSING	Revision of Ferry regulatory requirements.	Revision of requirements unlikely in the short term. Proposed score 3.

It has been claimed that France can export electricity to Britain cheaper than it can be produced in Britain, because such a high proportion of French electricty is produced by nuclear power.[67] There may also be differences in costing practices which account for part of the difference in price.

With the length of time it takes to build a major power station, the pattern of power station types is unlikely to change significantly by the end of the century or indeed in the next twenty years. The generating units are likely to be mainly in the 300MW(e) - 720MW(e) range.[68] However, there are signs of interest growing in power stations of 1GW(e) or more. Very rarely are two power stations exactly the same in every detail. Many factors introduce detailed changes, quite apart from the advances in technology that take place with time. These variations may have their origins in:- specific site conditions, material conditions changes in suppliers, component design changes and changes in operating conditions.

TABLE 27   CHANNEL CROSSING ECONOMIC FACTOR RANK
           SCORE OF PROPOSALS

PROPOSAL	ECONOMIC FACTOR CONCERNS	SCORE JUSTIFIED
EURO-BRIDGE	£5.9bn, no indication of possible variation.	No consideration of variation given. Proposed score 2.
EURO-ROUTE	£5.2bn. Proposer suggested total cost may reach £10.7bn (£7.2bn for the motorway link and £3.5bn for the rail link).	If variation in the range mentioned was realized the project would be unacceptable. Proposed score 3.
CHANNEL TUNNEL	Maximum debt the project would incur would be £4.75bn allowing £1bn for unforeseen contingencies.	This seems to include a reasonable allowance for contingencies. Proposed score 1.
CHANNEL EXPRESS WAY	£2.1bn excluding interest during construction and £2.5bn including construction period interest and fees. No discussion of variation.	Although this is the simplest scheme no allowance is made for cost variation. Proposed score 2.
NO FIXED LINK CROSSING	No costs are given, but for a comparable service new ferries and terminals would be required.	No figures given. Proposed score 2.

TABLE 28   CHANNEL CROSSING SOCIO-POLITICAL FACTOR RANK
           SCORE OF PROPOSALS

PROPOSAL	SOCIO-POLITICAL FACTOR CONCERNS	SCORE JUSTIFIED
EURO-BRIDGE	Changes in local environment and improvement in employment prospects. Risks to drivers on bridge.	No serious objection. Proposed score 1.
EURO-ROUTE	Changes in local environment and improvement in employment prospects. Adequacy of ventilation.	No serious objection. Proposed score 1.
CHANNEL TUNNEL	Changes in local environment and improvement in employment prospects. Adequacy of ventilation.	No serious objection. Proposed score 1.
CHANNEL EXPRESS WAY	Changes in local environment and improvement in employment prospects. Adequacy of ventilation.	No serious objection. Proposed score 1.
NO FIXED LINK CROSSING	Inadequate transport service.	Until service improves some objection. Proposed score 2.

TABLE 29   OVERALL RANKING OF THE ACCEPTABILITY OF
CHANNEL CROSSING PROPOSALS

PROPOSAL	TOTAL SCORE	RANK
EUROBRIDGE	5	2
EUROROUTE	6	2
CHANNEL TUNNEL	4	3
CHANNEL EXPRESSWAY	5	2
NO FIXED LINK OPTION	7	1

Regardless of the detail developments that take place the power stations are, for the reasons already mentioned, likely to be conventionally fuelled, nuclear fuelled and hydroelectric. English models for the form of conventional power stations could be:- the Drax coal fired station which currently consists of three 660MW units and the Littlebrook D oil fired station which also consists of three 660MW units. Currently British nuclear stations are gas cooled and so are rather different to the majority of the rest of the world, which uses light water reactors. However, the intention is to build a series of Pressurized Water Reactors of which the Sizewell 'B' reactor is the first. The Sizewell station will have a net electric output of 1175MW based on two turbine generators of 660MW capacity.[69]

Although there is a generic similarity between many of the reactors in use there are often many quite important differences between reactors nominally of the same type, for example there are many differences between French and German PWR's and the PWR proposed for Sizewell. There is an even greater diversity in the design of hydroelectric schemes, the nature of which makes each scheme different. The magnitude of the diversity of hydroelectric schemes is illustrated by the Dinorwig pumped storage power station and the proposal to use the tidal power from the Severn Estuary.[70][71]

Although there are some common features of public safety implications with each energy option, each option does tend to have its own specific safety considerations. In Table 30 special public safety considerations of each energy option are summarized. The options are summarized in terms of the energy source and the direct and indirect risks, direct risks being those resulting from using the source and indirect risks being those associated with winning and disposing of the source.

The description of the public safety considerations in Table 30 is qualitative and an indication of the relative importance of the various factors in quantitative terms is given in Table 31.

Public safety is not just simply a national matter, the international aspects are also very important. It is perhaps the international implications that underline the significance of some of the public

TABLE 30   PUBLIC SAFETY CONSIDERATIONS IN FUEL OPTIONS

OPTION	DIRECT PUBLIC SAFETY CONCERN	INDIRECT PUBLIC SAFETY CONCERN
COAL	Sulphur dioxide Lakes sterilised Benzo-pyrene (carcinogen)	Mining risks
OIL	Sulphur dioxide Nitrogen oxides Lakes sterilised	Oil rig risks
GAS	Sulphur dioxide Nitrogen oxides Lakes sterilised	Pipeline risks
NUCLEAR	Radiation Active waste disposal	Uranium mining Leaking of radioactivity
HYDRO-ELECTRIC	Flooding	Uncertainty of environmental impact epidemics

TABLE 31   PUBLIC SAFETY CONSIDERATION IN QUANTITATIVE TERMS

OPTION	PROBABILITY OF AN INDIVIDUAL DEATH YEAR	OTHER COMMENTS
FOSSIL FUEL	$0.2 - 4 \times 10^{-6}$ (72) Estimated from data	In 1962 it is claimed London smog caused 750 deaths.[72] Benzo pyrene released estimated to cause 4 to 8 times more deaths per gigawatt of electricity produced than nuclear power.[73]
NUCLEAR FUEL	1×10^{-6} Suggested regulatory limit	Nuclear waste is a smaller risk than coal ash.[74][75]
HYDRO-ELECTRIC	$1 - 5 \times 10^{-7}$(72)(73) based on average over whole population for UK and USA	Based on historical evidence the average frequency of dam failures in the UK is about 2×10^{-2} per year.[77] Dam failures can have significant consequences.

safety concerns.   These problems include the rising level of nitrate and sulphate in Greenland ice, and acid rain in Scandinavia and West Germany.   Some indication of the concern about these problems is shown by the fact that in Britain alone the Department of the Environment announced that it is to spend £600m reducing the emission of sulphur dioxide from three power stations.   Chernobyl is a particularly pertinent and large scale example of how failures at power stations can cause restrictions on the use of land and livestock in many countries other than that country in which the failure occurs.

In Table 32 some examples of the national and international concerns about public safety implications of power generation are summarized. Clearly the international concerns are more intense when the countries are close together, as in Europe.   The table should not be read in the pessimistic way that the situation is one that cannot be made acceptable.   Of course there is a discussion about the definition of what is acceptable, but by careful attention to siting, design and operation it is considered that each of the options can be made acceptable.

TABLE 32   NATIONAL AND INTERNATIONAL CONCERNS ABOUT
           PUBLIC SAFETY

OPTION	NATIONAL CONCERNS	INTERNATIONAL CONCERNS
FOSSIL FUEL	Greenhouse effect(CO_2) Ash Acid rain Changing conditions of streams and waters.	Greenhouse effect(CO_2) Acid rain Benzo-pyrene (carcinogen)
NUCLEAR FUEL	Radiation Release of radioactive material to the environment	Radiation Release and spread of radioactive material
HYDRO- ELECTRIC	Changes in local environment Flooding from failure	Cross border changes in local environment and flooding from failure

A Ranking of the acceptability of the options was built on a number of assumptions, which appear to be justified by the general pattern of power plant technical and economic data.   Assessing the Ranking of socio-political factors was based on the elaborate survey of public opinion on energy made for the Commission of the European Communities.[49]   The report showed that for the European Community as a whole there was most support for developing renewable energy, with conventional sources and energy saving next, developing nuclear energy fourth and importing electricity from abroad being judged to be the least attractive option.*   The findings of the survey are summarized

*In Europe there are several cases where electricity is traded between countries, for example Britain imports electricity from France by means of a cable laid under the English Channel.   Obviously such solutions are not open to every country.

in Table 33. It must be remembered that the table presents the lay preferences for the decision options and is in no way a technical or economic assessment of the optimum decision.

TABLE 33   PREFERRED SOLUTIONS AND PRIORITIES FROM EEC PUBLIC OPINION SURVEY

| | SOLUTION FOR ENERGY NEEDS TOTAL OF 1ST AND 2ND PREFERENCES | | | |
OPTION	LOWEST PRICE %	INDEPEND- ENCE %	MINIMISE POLLUTION %	OVERALL %
BUY FROM ABROAD	27	9	9	12
DEVELOP RENEWABLE ENERGY	61	74	80	71
DEVELOP NUCLEAR ENERGY	26	30	19	25
RETURN TO TRADITIONAL SOURCES	38	42	38	39
SAVE ENERGY	35	34	46	38
DON'T KNOW	4	3	2	5

The Ranking Scores of the Individual Factors and the overall Ranks considered to be justified are shown in Table 34. The economic advantages generally appear to be offset by the socio-political disadvantages. There is little or nothing to choose between the acceptability of the options. The question that is not considered is the availability of the options for a particular situation.

TABLE 34   OVERALL RANKING OF THE ENERGY OPTIONS

OPTION	TECHNICAL RANKING SCORE	ECONOMIC RANKING SCORE	SOCIO- POLITICAL RANKING SCORE	OVERALL RISK RANK
FOSSIL FUEL	1	1	1 1/2	3
NUCLEAR FUEL	1	3/4	2	3
HYDRO- ELECTRIC	1	1/2	1 1/2	3

While none of the case studies were perfect, when taken together they suggest that given appropriate evidence the Ranking Technique gives a defensible comparative assessment of the options. The structure of the Technique also gives a more logical assessment of the options than an assessment based simply on consideration of one factor alone.

Chapter 9

The Basis for Alternatives to the Ranking Technique in the Decision Making Process

This chapter aims to assess the basis for possible alternatives to the Ranking Technique. The intention is not to examine alternative techniques, as these have already been reviewed in Chapter 3, but to examine what could rather grandiosely be described as the philosophical basis for alternatives. Running through this assessment is the view that regardless of whether the knowledge is subjective or objective there is unlikely to be absolute certainty. In all parts of the argument allowance has to be made for uncertainty. This in a way is recognition of the fact that all knowledge is evolutionary. The first part of the assessment considers the basis for qualitative alternatives and the second part of the assessment considers the basis for quantitative alternatives and finally a number of conclusions are drawn about the justification for alternatives.

Before starting the assessment a few introductory remarks are necessary to identify more clearly the standpoint from which the assessment is made and the nature of the environment it is assumed surrounds and influences risk acceptability decision making. The standpoint assumed is that the analysis of acceptability that has to be made must be capable of demonstrating publicly that all risks have been judged fairly on a uniform and consistent basis. The criteria that have been postulated have been put forward in a way that enables them to be used generally for assessing comprehensive acceptability of risks. It is appreciated that as the concept of comprehensive assessment is intended to span all aspects of risk special criteria might have to be developed for some applications of the Ranking Technique. For analytical purposes it is considered appropriate to group the various factors that have to be considered under the headings of technical, economic and socio-political as used in the Ranking Technique. As the aim is to assess the comprehensive acceptability in a fair almost legal way one legal maxim is adopted, namely 'de minimis non curat'. In other words the law is not concerned with trifles. In the context of this assessment this means that attention is concentrated on the overall effectiveness of the Technique in determining the acceptability of a proposal.

Having identified the standpoint from which the assessment is made, attention is drawn to the fact that we all live in an ever changing environment. In the terms of this assessment the ever changing environment has six important features that must be allowed for. These features are:- public perception of risk acceptability changes with time, scientific knowledge about the significance of risks changes with time, knowledge about how risks can be reduced changes with time, legal requirements for dealing with risk change with time, needs for particular activities change with time and acceptable working patterns change with time. Not all six features will be relevant to every decision making situation.

The fact that this ever changing environment has to be allowed for in this assessment exposes the range of interactions that have to be considered. One way this ever changing environment influences the assessment is by the fact that it generates the question 'are these criteria appropriate to these circumstances?'. A particularly important target for this question is in a relation to the appropriateness of the techniques for determining the acceptability of the risks associated with novel, new and untried plant.

QUALITATIVELY BASED ALTERNATIVES

Establishing a risk acceptability criteria of the form proposed in earlier chapters is not intended to stop progress, but the quantitative basis of the proposed criteria does mean that concomitant quantitative evidence is ultimately required to justify acceptability. When new developments start comprehensive reliable quantitative evidence may not be available. This means that for novel developments a qualitative base may have to be the starting point for the evolution of adequate evidence of acceptability. So although a qualitative alternative to the proposed criteria may not be acceptable as the ultimate criteria it may be accepted as being or helpful in some preliminary stages before all the quantitative data required for complete justification is fully generated. This difference between qualitative and quantitative data is important and is sometimes obscured. In the sense used in this study qualitative data is based on opinion and quantitative data is based on measurement. Because of the difference in the two types of data it is worth defining the capability and limits of qualitative techniques.

If the evidence available is only in a qualitative form confidence in the validity of the arguments presented can be maximized by logical structured analysis. There are five essential steps in the structured analysis of qualitative evidence.[4] The steps are:- 1) Reduction of the information available to a consistent manageable form. 2) Finding a way of displaying the information. 3) Determining what conclusions the information indicates. 4) Assessing the confidence that can be associated with the conclusions. 5) Making it clear what new information is required and how it can be incorporated in the analysis.

To prevent misunderstanding it must be stressed that structuring the analysis of qualitative data does not convert it into quantitative data, but it improves understanding of its significance and provides a logical base from which it is possible to iterate towards a quantitative understanding. It is suggested that the most effective progress towards a logically defensible judgement about the acceptability of the risks associated with a novel project can best be made if the procedure summarized in Table 35 is followed. It is appreciated computer programs exist for helping perform such procedure. The procedure outlined being vital when there is only qualitative evidence available. The essential features of the procedure are: emphasis on determining and testing the quality of the evidence obtained, determination of the gaps in the evidence and determination of the action that has to be taken to obtain the additional evidence that is seen to be required to demonstrate the acceptability criteria are satisfied.

TABLE 35 PROCEDURE FOR ANALYSIS OF QUALITATIVE EVIDENCE

STEP NUMBER	NATURE OF STEP	OPTIMUM RESULT	ADDITIONAL ACTION
1	Define the risk	The risk is defined comprehensively	If the risk cannot be defined comprehensively further study is required
2	Identify criteria to be satisfied	This should simply be endorsing the adopting of the universal or partial criteria proposed in this study	It is possible that in some unique circumstances special criteria would have to be devised
3	Collection of relevant data or advice	Cross-checking the data or advice from several sources confirms the evidence	Further search required if adequate evidence not found
4	Structure data obtained. This includes the five subroutines: 1) Put data in consistent form 2) Display data 3) Determine conclusions 4) Assess confidence in conclusions 5) Identify new information required	Data found to be reliable and consistent and the need for new information clearly and accurately defined	Fill in gaps in data and improve relevance and quality of data
5	Weigh evidence obtained	A particular weighting is found to be justified	Refine and improve data until an acceptable weighting is obtained

The essential conclusion that is suggested by this examination of the possible use that can be made of qualitative evidence is that its role is limited by the fact that it cannot be converted directly into quantitatve evidence. The most that can be expected from qualitative evidence is that it includes:consistent expert opinion about the risks associated with a proposal, a description of the nature of the risks and a statement of how the required quantitative justification of acceptability of the risks will be obtained. Qualitative evidence is no substitute for quantitative evidence. In a subject like risk acceptability qualitative arguments can,and generally do, expose a lack of acceptable alternative. But carefully structured analysis of qualitative evidence can be helpful in identifying the optimum procedure to be followed to develop the quantitative evidence required to prove the acceptability of the risks involved in a proposal.

One special role for a qualitative description of acceptablity is when acceptability has been determined quantitatively and it is necessary, perhaps for political reasons, to describe justification for a proposal being acceptable to a non-technical audience in qualitative non-dimensional terms.

QUANTITATIVELY BASED ALTERNATIVES

There are several ways risk can be measured in quantitative terms, so clearly there are several units that risk acceptability criteria can be expressed in. One part of the expression of risk has to stay in fairly constant terms and that is the probability that adverse conditions will occur in a specific unit of time. A unit time of a year is widely accepted and it is not subject to any great controversy. However, when assessing the overall benefit of a proposal all the adverse conditions that may arise throughout its life must be integrated, so perhaps the life of a proposal is the more appropriate unit.

The other part of the risk expression is the subject of some debate. The most direct way of expressing the risk is to put it, as has been proposed for the cases considered in this study, as the risk of an unacceptable condition arising and some kind of loss being generated. Other closely related ways could be to define the risk of a specific number of people, say ten, being killed or of there being a specific number of casualties. Rather more remote ways of specifying the risk would be: to express it in terms of the probability of a release of toxic material or an accident involving costs of a certain level measured in terms of the cost of loss of lives and damage to property. It is possible that for some applications the technical risk aspects could simply be described by an index of technical worth. Such an approach would in some ways be a variation of the Risk Reduction method described in Chapter 3. The problem would be how worth should be measured. One possible solution would be to measure worth in terms of the probability of a plant performing as specified for a particular length of time.

It has to be appreciated that describing potential loss in money terms is a procedure that is familiar to the insurance market and underwriters. However, to the general public describing loss of life and limb in money terms can sometimes be considered as callous and mercenary. This point was brought out by the way the press dealt with the negligence case brought against the Ford Motor Company about the safety characteristics of their Pinto model. The press objected strongly to the cost-benefit approach to safety.[20] With an emotive subject like risk acceptability the importance of presenting the evidence in a simple, honest, neutral way must not be overlooked. For this reason, it is suggested that defining acceptability of risk in money terms, which involved some correlation being made between money and the value of life is inappropriate for general public presentation. Also expressing risk in money terms can lead to complications due to the purchasing value of money changing significantly in relatively short periods, which can quickly make the description out of date. Further comparison of risk between countries can be difficult because of changes in exchange rates make the comparison of risk difficult. Regardless of the difficulty the assessment of the economic aspects of a proposal has to take account of all economic gains and losses likely throughout the life of the proposal.

This brings the argument back to including in the description of loss the number of people killed or hurt. It could be argued that this is also callous, but it is clear and it can be compared with the other risks people are exposed to and that they expose themselves to. In making such comparisons care has to be taken to ensure that like is compared with like and that the quantitative values used in the comparison are valid. For this reason it is considered that describing the risk in terms of the probability of an individual in the area of concern being killed is the fairest and most honest way of the criteria defining the acceptability of the risk. To describe the risk in terms of groups of people being killed would be slightly more emotive. One problem with the definition that remains is, does being killed mean only death at the time the adverse event occurs or does it include those that die later. In this study it is arbitrarily assumed that an assessment should be based on all the additional deaths that may arise from the lifetime operation of the proposals.

The specific application to nuclear power plants is an example of an application that may need a more refined means of defining acceptability, particularly where large accidents are concerned. The concept of a "social risk" was introduced by Sir Frank Layfield in the Sizewell 'B' public inquiry and must be included. This was mentioned in Chapter 5 and is addressed further in Chapters 10 and 11. The case of the nuclear industry serves to illustrate how the criteria used may have to be tailored to a specific application but underlines the need for consistency in the criteria to ensure comparability. In addition to the cases where it is appropriate to measure the technical and economic aspects of risk in terms of people being killed or hurt proposals may arise in which the risk is measured purely in terms of some loss of convenience. Criteria for Ranking such proposals can also be devised.

Another feature of the Technique that is open to discussion is whether the degrees of acceptability should be described in steps or as part of a continuous line or as a simple point. Identifying four steps in the criteria, as in the proposed criteria, is about the optimum number of steps that can be accepted. Three steps would be too coarse and more than four steps would give a misleading degree of refinement. This division into only four steps is, perhaps, also defensible on the basis of the de minimis principle and the fact that in the Netherlands they found it convenient for the selection of electrical equipment to operate in areas where there is a risk of a gas explosion to identify four types of potentially hazardous zone.[77] Further justification of a small number of Ranking steps is given by the fact that in Britain the Department of the Environment ask the Health and Safety Executive to grade their advice on the acceptability of planning proposals into one of three grades which are: negligible risk, marginal risk and substantial risk.[78] Also pollution of rivers is categorized into four classes: class 1 for unpolluted, class 2 for doubt, class 3 for poor and class 4 for grossly polluted rivers. The eleven divisions of the Richter Scale and the thirteen divisions of the Beaufort Scale can perhaps be defended on the basis that they only categorize a single variable that can be measured fairly accurately.

Defining the steps in the criteria in the way that it has been proposed allows in a direct way for uncertainty in the evidence likely to be available. For each step the associated probabilities are broad banded in the middle and open ended for the top and bottom steps. The advantage of this definition of the steps is that it gives the proposer a clear target to aim at. The steps could have been defined in more sophisticated statistical terms, but such a presentation would also tend to make the public acceptability of the criteria questionable.

CONCLUSIONS

The examination of the possible basis for alternatives to the proposed comprehensive risk acceptability Ranking criteria has suggested the following conclusions:-

1)   As the Ranking Technique is conceived as presenting a defensible non-dimensional interpretation of a quantified justification of the acceptability of a proposal there is no alternative to ultimately basing the Ranking on quantitative knowledge. However, in the initial stages of a novel project it may be useful to start building up confidence about the degree to which the criteria will be satisfied by assessing relevant qualitative data or subjective opinions. In making use of such qualitative data an attempt must be made to relate the data to the quantitative steps defined in the criteria. Such a process does not require different criteria.

2)   The quantitative criteria proposed cannot be replaced by or satisfied by qualitative data, attempting to satisfy quantitative criteria in qualitative terms could be interpreted as exposing a lack of definitive knowledge about the proposal.

3)   It is appreciated that for judging the acceptability of proposals that do not involve risk in terms of people being killed or hurt it would be appropriate to devise technical and economic criteria

that simply measure risk in terms of loss of convenience or loss of performance.

4)   The steps in the criteria seem to be the optimum compromise between detailed categorization and a broad go or no-go division. Also the steps in the categorization do to some extent make appropriate allowance for the likely uncertainty associated with estimates of compliance with each Ranking level.

5)   The way in which the component of time is written into the criteria could be more clearly defined. It is assumed that when an assessment of acceptability is made the decision maker will have in mind the lifetime acceptability of the proposal. On this basis it is clear the Ranking should be made on the basis of lifetime acceptability.

Chapter 10

Guidelines for the Application of the Ranking Technique

The earlier chapters demonstrated the nature of the Ranking Technique and how it could be used as an aid to decision making. The technique was designed initially for comprehensive assessment of the acceptability of decision options involving potentially hazardous technology projects such as nuclear power plants or chemical plants. Although designed for comprehensive assessment the technique can be used in a partial way either to assess one aspect of a project or to assess the characteristics of project options in a particular way. In other words the technique can be helpful with a whole matrix of decision evaluation situations.

The Layfield report showed how with a major project like a nuclear power plant there may be lack of guidance about how decisions on one aspect like risk acceptability should be made.[79] Risk acceptability guidance was not the only aspect of determining the acceptability of a project that the Layfield report exposed where the Ranking Technique could be useful. The Layfield report also showed that the structure of the management of the licensing process was unpredictable and had serious shortcomings.[80] Among these shortcomings was a lack of definition of the criteria for judging acceptability.[81] The Layfield report merely exposes weaknesses in the decision making process associated with a major project like a nuclear power reactor, similar concerns apply to decision making in general no matter whether it is related to a research and development programme or a fully automated sausage-roll factory.

The general procedure to be followed in using the Ranking Technique is show diagrammatically in Fig. 6 in the form of a flow diagram. Six stages in the procedure are identified. Stage 1 is definition of the decision requirement, this is important as often at the beginning of a decision making process the nature of the decision required and the options to be considered are not clear. Stage 2 requires definition of the criteria to be used for judging and scoring the acceptability of each factor in the decision making process. Stages 3, 4 and 5 are evaluation of the data available and determination of the Ranking justified. The evaluation processes are not described here as their nature has already been discussed in Chapters 5, 6 and 7. It only need be said that the processes used must be defensible and thorough, as they are the basis on which the options are Ranked they may be subject to critical examination to determine the confidence that can be placed in the Ranking. In stage 6 the decision is taken about which decision option is most acceptable. It may be that the first attempt to Rank the options is unsatisfactory because the evidence is too weak, in such cases the evidence has to be improved so that the quality of the Ranking can be refined until it is satisfactory.

In the rest of this chapter the questions about the application of the Ranking Technique that are examined are: what use can be made of the Technique, who can use the Technique, what input is required, what output is expected and what is the overall view of Ranking. The aim

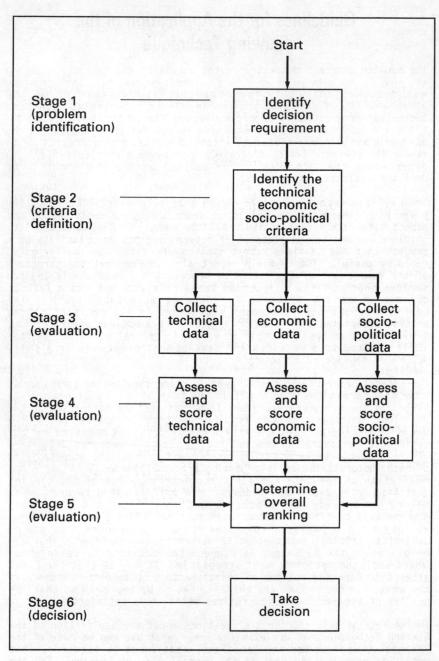

Fig 6 Ranking decision

being to generate guidelines for the effective exploitation of the Technique. The very nature of the discussion requires that some examination of the way the Ranking Technique may be used in conjunction with other Decision Making aids.

USE OF THE RANKING TECHNIQUE

In its simplest and most general applications the Technique provides a logical structure for the assessment of any decision problem. Logical structuring being the first step in building up the analysis of any issues. The very process of structuring the analysis of a particular problem normally exposes more clearly not only the result that it is hoped solving the problem will produce but the adequacy of available knowledge for solving the problem. The fact that the Technique aims to make a comprehensive assessment of the technical, economic and socio-political aspects of a proposition means that the structuring is inherently multi-disciplinary. It should not be forgotten that the Technique may also be used just for single discipline analysis when required.

This basic problem structuring capability of the Technique can be used for structuring assessment of decisions involving major technical projects, research and development programmes, risk acceptability issues, company organisation, company strategy and investment plans.

The second stage of the application of the Technique arises as the understanding of the problem becomes more refined and allows a critical assessment to be made of the criteria that should be used to assess and weight the significance of each factor. Determination of criteria and weighting of significance requires a critical informed judgement to be made about how the validity of the Ranking of each factor can be justified. In each distinct application of the Technique the criteria may be different. Although there may be families of applications where the pattern of the criteria may be essentially the same. For example it would be difficult to conceive of the criteria used for judging the acceptability of various major industrial risks being different, but the criteria for judging the of efficacy for different kinds of investment may be different. Equally the criteria for judging which research and development programme to choose may be different for specific topics and they also may be quite different from the criteria used for judging other forms of investment. The important function of the Technique is that it requires criteria to be specified in a consistent and logical way.

In the evaluation stage of the application of the Technique, which aims to determine how well the criteria are satisfied an assessment of the data and evaluation of the analytical methods which may be used are required. Both the data and the methods of analysis must be relevant. Evaluation of the relevance of the data gives an indication of the accuracy with which satisfaction of the criteria can be determined. The accuracy with which satisfaction of the criteria can be determined will vary considerably, being very high when the project is one of a series which have been comprehensively tested. When the project is novel and untested the uncertainty will be considerable. This problem has to be faced by the builders of any novel plant or equipment. All the Technique does is to identify what data must be obtained and expose what the significance of the data is likely to be. In some ways with novel plant or equipment this data requirement determines the research and development programme required.

The civil aircraft industry has done more than many industries to codify the design of testing procedures. An example of the detail of the Joint Airworthiness Requirements for All Weather Operations is given by the requirement that flight demonstrations of flight path and speed control should show that 95% of demonstration approaches meet the following criteria[82]:-

a) The approach from 150m is completed without a system failure.
b) Between 150m and the start of flare, the speed should be maintained within $\pm$ 5 knots of the approach speed (disregarding rapid airspeed fluctuations associated with turbulence) under all intended flight conditions.
c) The position of the aeroplane should be such that between 90m and the decision height the deviations with regard to the reference Instrument Landing System (ILS) beam should not exceed the values of glide path or localizer deviation established for the excess-deviation alerts.

It is also important to note that the number of demonstration approaches should be such that a 90% confidence level that the criteria are satisfied can be established. Two methods of anlaysis of the results of the demonstration flights are allowed by the requirements. One method, the 'Pass or Fail' method, is based on the Poisson distribution. According to this distribution it is possible to determine the number of approaches which have to be made as a function of the number of go-arounds to show compliance with the 95% success rate with a confidence level of 90%. The Requirements include a diagram which shows the accepted relationship between: number of approaches, number of failed approaches and the acceptability of the performance. The other method of analysis is called the 'Continuous Method' and for the measurements made predicts the confidence level of the probability that the variable of interest does not exceed the specified threshold value. Theoretical justification of the method is based on assuming that the experimental measurements can be related to a form of Gaussian distribution.

Returning to the specific question of what use can be made of the Ranking Technique, many decisions are not as codified as determining the acceptability of the airworthiness of an aeroplane from the results of a flight test programme. As mentioned earlier it was formally recognized in the Layfield report that there was lack of guidance about how decisions like the acceptability of nuclear plant should be made. The Ranking Technique can be used to make such decisions in a consistent way. For any decisions that have to be made on a comprehensive basis, as explained earlier, the three questions that have to be answered are what are the technical, economic and socio-political criteria that have to be satisfied. If for some reason the decision is limited to only one or two features of a problem such as the technical and/or the economic factors the Ranking Technique can still be used, by just basing the Ranking on those factors. The Ranking in such a case is clearly not a comprehensive Ranking, but a mono- or bi- factor Ranking.

As already mentioned, at the beginning of an assessment the data on which the assessment has to be based may be weak. It may be that the Ranking has at first to be based on qualitative data, because the project is novel and there is no quantitative data, the data there is must be put into the most logically defensible form possible. The necessary process has already been discussed in Chapter 9 but a few specific comments are appropriate to this discussion of the use of the Ranking Technique. Qualitative data often has its origins in expert opinion. Even before any attempt is made to order the data it has to be recognized that the expert opinions may have been collected in an unstructured almost random way and the experts may not even have been asked the same questions. This draws attention to the fact that the quality of the information depends to a considerable extent on the way it is collected. To ensure that the quality of the information collected is as high as possible several rules can be postulated. The rules are (83)(84):-

1) The experts consulted should have expertise in the field being studied.
2) Experts should actively try and identify evidence that tends to contradict their initial opinions.
3) The problems on which expert opinion is sought should be kept down to an understandable size.
4) Analysis of the views of several experts is better than the view of a single expert.
5) Structured elicitation of opinions is better than unstructured questioning.
6) Mathematical analysis of opinions is better than some subjective view of opinion.

The conclusion that appears to be justified is that the Ranking Technique can be used as an aid for a wide variety of decision making purposes. It can be used in either the comprehensive form or the mono- or bi- factor form. For each application of the Technique appropriate and consistent criteria must be established. The accuracy of the scoring for Ranking each factor against the criteria adopted depends on the quality of the information available. The variations in quality ranging from qualitative data based on assessment of expert opinion to accurate quantitative data derived from measurements and observations on many similar cases. Preliminary Ranking based on less than perfect data can be iteratively improved as better data becomes available. With the passage of time, as with most things in life, there may be may changes to the data that necessitate modification of the Ranking. In building up a Ranking for a novel project for which there is no data an initial impression can often be built up using qualitative data derived from expert opinion. The use of such qualitative data can be justified if the rules to maximize data quality, outlined above, are followed. Qualitative data based Ranking must never be confused with Ranking based on quantitative data, the two Rankings are quite different. Qualitative data based Ranking is really only of use in preliminary decision making. Such use of the Ranking Technique is important, as it has the benefit of giving the assessment a logical and consistent structure.

WHO SHOULD USE THE RANKING TECHNIQUE

Although the question of who should use the Ranking Technique has been answered indirectly in the previous section, in this section the problem of identifying the specific types of decision maker who could with benefit use the Ranking Technique is examined. The enormous range of decision types was discussed in Chapter 2. Similarly the range of types of decision maker is enormous they range from: the plant manager who has to determine what the output should be of the plant he is responsible for to the senior politician who has to decide whether or not public expenditure on a particular project is justified. Between these two extremes is a whole range of decision makers some of whom interact with each other in the decision making process. The interactions also have many forms, they may involve one group of decision makers advising another set of decision makers about what form a decision should take or at the other extreme it may involve one decision maker instructing another decision maker within what limits he can make decisions.

From the very broad range of decision makers that exist several types can be identified, they can with some advantage be divided into: comprehensive, technical, economic and socio-political groups in a similar way to Ranking Technique itself. Each group has its own characteristics and objectives, which define how appropriate it is for them to use the Ranking Technique. The characteristics and objectives of each group of decision makers can be related to the size and scope of the decisions they are responible for. Starting from the way the nature of simple and comprehensive decisions is described in Tables 2 and 3 and Chapter 2. Tables 36 and 37 have been constructed to show how the various groups of decision maker are related to decisions of different complexities. Table 36 deals with simple decisions and Table 37 deals with complex decisions.

The tables also show how the needs of different types of decision maker vary. The nature of the role of comprehensive decision makers identified endorses the view that the comprehensive version of the Ranking Technique, which takes account of the technical, economic and socio-political factors should be a useful aid to such decision makers. This means that anyone who could be identified as a comprehensive decision maker could with benefit use the Ranking Technique to supplement his decision making procedure. The type of people that come under this heading are managers, government officials at local, national and international levels and politicians. Each decision maker's use of the Technique may be different and the criteria for Ranking and weighting each factor may have to be tailored to suit each family of applications. In cases where the Ranking forms part of some open exchange with the public it is essential that the criteria adopted are used in a consistent way and that the evidence used for Ranking can be justified. If the criteria used for a particular family of decisions are not consistent the possibility of comparing Ranking is destroyed.

TABLE 36   CLASSIFICATION OF DECISION MAKERS FOR
SIMPLE DECISIONS

	EXAMPLES OF DECISION MAKERS IN EACH GROUP			
SCOPE OF DECISION	COMPRE-HENSIVE	TECHNICAL	ECONOMIC	SOCIO-POLITICAL
ORGANIZA-TIONAL	Manager who decides which system should be adopted	Design Engineer who decides specification of pump to be bought	Finance Officer who decides if funds are available for purchase of pump	Manager who decides how any trade or union regulations are to be satisfied
NATIONAL	Someone who agrees a certain product should be marketed nationally	Someone responsible for agreeing a national technical standard	Someone responsible for agreeing a national research budget on a particular topic	Someone responsible for ensuring that a proper procedure is established for determing public acceptability of a project
INTER-NATIONAL	Someone who decides an organization should operate in several countries	An engineer responsible for obtaining international approval of a piece of equipment	Someone responsible for agreeing how the budget of an international organization will be divided	Someone responsible for assessing opinion on a certain project in several countries
REGULA-TORY	An inspector who decides if use of a particular material should be banned	Inspector deciding if a particular piece of equipment satisfies regulations	An inspector who decides expenditure on a particular study contract is justified	Inspector deciding if some consultation with other parties is required

TABLE 37 CLASSIFICATION OF DECISION MAKERS FOR COMPLEX DECISIONS

SCOPE OF DECISION	EXAMPLES OF DECISION MAKERS IN EACH GROUP			
	COMPRE-HENSIVE	TECHNICAL	ECONOMIC	SOCIO-POLITICAL
ORGANIZA-TIONAL	Someone who decides which plant should be built and where	An Engineer who approves the overall specifica-tion of a plant	Someone responsible for raising the funding for a major project	Someone responsible for discuss-ing hazard implications with the public
NATIONAL	Someone who agrees there should be government support for a proprosal	An Engineer responsible for specify-ing the technical form of a national service such as a tele-phone system or an electricity distribution system	Someone responsible for allocat-ing the budget of a major Government Department such as the Ministry of Defence	Someone responsible for obtaining political support for a project
INTER-NATIONAL	Someone who agrees there should be inter-national support for a proposal	An Engineer responsible for the technical specifica-tion of some inter-national activity like trans-port of hazardous goods or air transport	Someone responsible for the allocation of funds of an inter-national body like the UN or the EEC	Someone responsible for the political negotiations of an inter-national project like the Channel Tunnel
REGULA-TORY	A regulatory Official who decides a major project cannot be approved	Inspector deciding if a particular plant satisfies regulations	Someone who decides a regulatory department should have a certain budget	Inspector deciding if consulta-tion with interested parties has been adequate

For decision makers concerned with just technical, economic or socio-political issues they can use the appropriate part of the Ranking Technique to supplement and perhaps even structure their decision making.

The conclusion that appears justified about who should use the Ranking Technique is that the full form of the Technique is most likely to be useful to those decision makers who have to make decisions in a comprehensive way, taking account of all the factors involved. The main benefits that the Technique should be to them are a consistent structuring their analysis of the options, identification of the criteria and improving comparability of assessment of options. Identification of the criteria is useful to all involved with the decision making as it clarifies for all concerned the targets to be aimed at and the basis for decision making.

Using the Ranking Technique in the partial form implies a use of the Technique that is subsidiary to the comprehensive use of the Technique, so the user is likely to be subsidiary to the comprehensive decision maker. However, in one important way the benefits of using the Ranking Technique in the partial form will be the same as using it in the comprehensive form namely structuring the argument and clarifying the targets aimed at. Also it will facilitate the construction of a comprehensive assessment, if such an assessment is required later.

INPUT REQUIRED

Ideally the input required would be accurate statistics directly related to each factor that has to be taken into account. In practice the data that is likely to be available may range from qualitative opinion to good quantitative statistics about for which the confidence limits are properly established. The problems of decision making are greatest when the data is poor, but this is just the time when decisions are usually most urgently required.

Taking the definition of the input required stage by stage. The first stage is to define the precise form of the Ranking Technique that is appropriate to the specific decision process. The second stage is to identify the criteria that are to be used for Ranking the various factors involved and the weight that is to be given to the significance of each factor that has to be integrated to give the overall Ranking. Defining the criteria that have to be used leads directly to the third stage, in the identification of the inputs required, which is identification and acquisition of the data required. The fourth stage is to evaluate the data and determine the Ranking justified.

The third stage of identification and acquisition of data is the topic that is concentrated on here, as the other stages are to a large extent problem specific and defined by the problem. Having identified the techniques and criteria to be used the search for data starts. With a novel project there may initially be no appropriate quantitative data and the decision has to be made on the basis of expert judgements. Judgements are by their very nature qualitative, but as already mentioned some procedures can be adopted to improve the usefulness of such information. The first step in the process is to structure how the expert judgements are made and collected. Earlier in the chapter the rules to be followed to ensure that the opinions derived from consultation with experts are of as high a quality as possible, so they need not be repeated here. All that need be emphasized is that no matter how well the structuring and analysis of expert opinion is arranged it still remains qualitative data. Where decisions are based on qualitative data the need to monitor and review such decisions as better data becomes available and better understanding of the issue develops is of paramount importance. Statistical analysis of the opinions expressed by experts should indicate the consistency of the opinions expressed. With all due respect to the experts involved the opinions will be fuzzy. Some views on how fuzzy data may be handled were given in Chapter 3. The form of analysis described by Unwin in reference 85 might also help in determining the quality of expert judgements.

The conclusion about the input required to the Ranking Technique is that it is the specific use of the Technique that determines the input required and it is the quality of the input that determines the quality of the Ranking and its usefulness. When the quality of the input is poor the basis for a decision is poor and the Ranking must be kept under review and adjusted to take account of better data as they become available.

OUTPUT EXPECTED

The output of the application of the Ranking Technique is an assessment of the decision options. The Ranking of the options may, provided adequate information is available, give the decision maker sufficient information to judge which option of the range of options will give the most rewarding payoff. In complex cases where there are many options to consider it may be helpful to display the Rankings on a variation of the Buckley[86] form of decision matrix or payoff matrix (as mentioned in Chapter 3) an example of such a display is shown in Figure 7. The construction of Figure 7 is based on the risk acceptability Ranking of a hypothetical potentially hazardous plant. Four design options are postulated and with each design option four possible levels of investment are postulated. The result is a matrix of sixteen possible options. Simply to demonstrate the use of a matrix display a Rank was assessed for each option. Seven of the assumed Ranks were rated likely to be acceptable without restriction. Of the seven acceptable without restriction options one can be seen to be acceptable even with the lowest level of investment.

In practice different options may be considered and the range of investment levels may not be the critical criteria, it may be the return on investment or public opinion or some other feature. Sometimes it may also be that the criteria used for Ranking are considered to be variable and that the different Rankings obtained with different criteria are the critical range of variables to be considered.

Essentially for either a comprehensive or partial Ranking the output

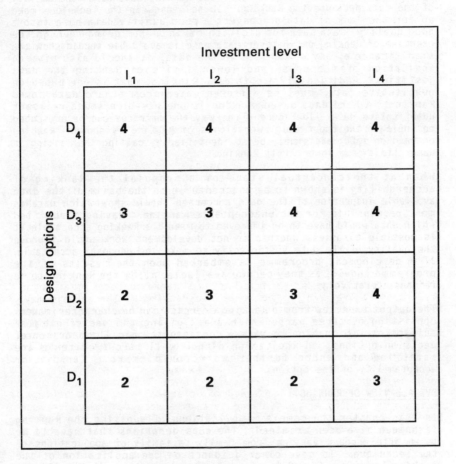

Fig 7 Matrix of ranking results

the Ranking Technique gives a decision maker is an assessment of how far the various associated factors satisfy the criteria that have been postulated. In this sense the Ranking is a summary of all the assessments that have been made in the evaluation of the proposal. As already mentioned the quality of the Ranking depends on the quality of the data put into the Ranking. In no sense can the Technique make up for the lack of data or convert a poor quality data base into a good quality data base for decision making. But going through the exercise of Ranking on whatever data base is available should show the significance of any weaknesses in the data, it should also give an indication of the upper and lower limits of Ranking the data justifies. Additionally a soft data Ranking, that is one based on qualitative data, must be differentiated from a hard data based Ranking. A hard data based Ranking is one based on sound relevant quantitative data. In Figure 8 the way the matrices can be presented to indicate the upper and lower limits of Ranking is shown. Ranking on hard or soft data simply being identified by calling the Ranking an upper limit or a lower limit Ranking.

When at the conceptual stage of a proposal the Ranking of acceptability is shown to be unacceptable on the basis of the data available inspection of the data concerned should show which data is most responsible for the unacceptable Ranking. Having identified which data would have to be improved to make the Ranking acceptable it is possible to assess whether or not development work would improve the quality of the data sufficiently to make the proposal acceptable. If a development programme is embarked upon the results of the programme should, as they become available, allow the Ranking to be refined iteratively.

The output expected from a Ranking exercise can be characterized as consisting of three parts which are: giving the decision maker sufficient information to make a consistent logical comparison of decision options, an indication of how well target criteria are satisfied and where further work could improve Ranking or acceptability of the options.

OVERALL VIEW OF RANKING

In this chapter the complex implications of applying the Ranking Technique have been examined. The considerations that have to be taken into account varying from family to family of applications of the Technique. To give clear guidance on the application of the Ranking Technique Fig. 9 is presented to show diagrammatically the influence of variation in data quality on determination of acceptability Ranks. The terms hard and soft data are used to describe upper and lower limits of data quality. Hard data is perfect defect free quantitative data that is directly relevant to the proposition being assessed. Soft data is qualitative data of doubtful validity or relevance. In practice neither perfect hard data nor completely soft data are likely to be available and some compromise has to be made about the data used, but the quality of the data available should improve as the proposal progresses. When a spectrum of options have been assessed using data with known limits of uncertainty the Ranking results can be clearly displayed in the matrix

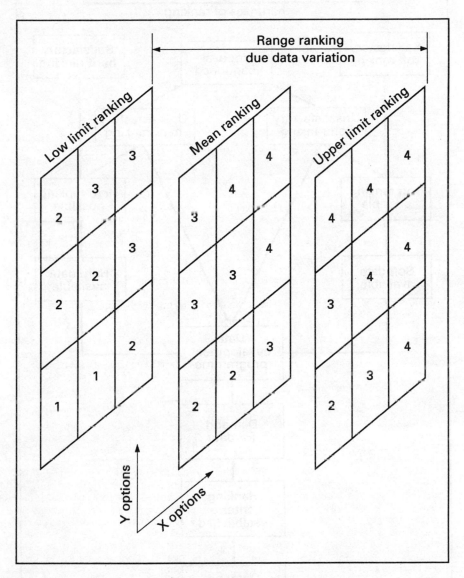

Fig 8 Ranking matrix limits

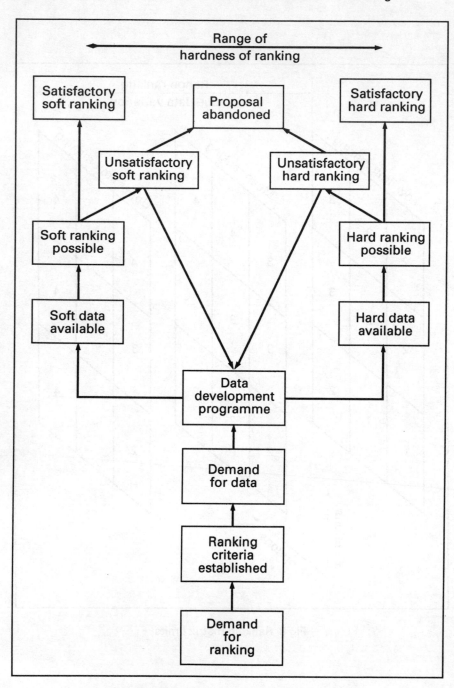

Fig 9 Ranking technique application flowsheet

form shown in Fig. 8, which makes clear the implication of the degree of uncertainty. One possibility Fig. 9 does not show is the possibility that during the Ranking process it might be considered that revision of the Ranking criteria is justified.

Chapter 11
Conclusions

In this study a coherent approach to the development of criteria for ranking complex technical project decisions was discussed. Although the Ranking Technique can be applied to any type of project from major research projects to siting a power station and from building a chemical plant to construction of a major tunnel attention was concentrated on decisions related to the acceptability of potentially hazardous plants. First the nature of potentially hazardous systems was assessed to provide the basis for the discussion of the suitability of the criteria proposed. Then a model with the essential features of a hazardous system was proposed; the model consisted of:- a risk source term, a control system, a containment system and the environment in which the potentially hazardous system has to operate. Next the risk based criteria currently used in five European countries were briefly reveiwed. This review showed there was considerable diversity in the criteria used. The feature most common in the criteria considered is that regulatory bodies tend to reserve their position by not specifying firm quantitative technical targets that have to be satisfied. At the same time it is recognized that regulatory bodies are increasingly couching their guidance about what will be considered acceptable in terms of a target hazard band which expresses the relationship between acceptable and unacceptable in terms of the probability of an accident occurring that will cause a certain number of fatalities. The band being one way of allowing for uncertainty in the estimate of risk and introducing a certain amount of flexibility in any associated decision making. A single point target is unrealistic to the extent that with any major project there are likely to be a whole spectrum of possible outcomes of an accident not just one unique outcome. Attention is drawn to the fact that the authorities in the Netherlands appear to have made the greatest step towards establishing a regulatory quantitative target that relates the acceptability of risks for all types of potentially hazardous fixed installations, to the probable number of fatalities and also incorporates a band to allow for uncertainty by leaving the action to reduce risk optional.

From the review of the various proposed technical quantitative targets a technical risk Ranking criteria was developed as part of the comprehensive risk Ranking technique. The criteria expressed acceptability in terms of the individual risk of death per year. When the risk is close to a less than 1 in 1,000,000 per year it is considered acceptable without restriction. When the risk is of the order or higher than 1 in 100,000 per year detailed evaluation of acceptability would be required. Risks of the order of 1 in 10,000 per year it is postulated would only be acceptable under very special circumstances and when the risk is close to greater than 1 in 1,000 per year it would be quite unacceptable.

From the overall criteria it was proposed that partial criteria covering sub-systems could be developed. The precise nature of the partial criteria depending on the nature and complexity of the particular project. In general the partial criteria that components or sub-systems or a complete project must be such that the total risk associated with all the partial criteria involved is, when integrated in an appropriate way, equal to or less than the risk allowed by the overall criteria.

In considering the implications of the criteria at the design, regulatory and operational level the following points were exposed as warranting emphasis:- 1) The design must be such that no feasible failures or events should result in a breach of the overall acceptability criteria. 2) If the people living in the area of the proposed plant will be exposed to a risk higher than would be considered acceptable by the proposed criteria the Regulatory Authority would have no alternative but to call for additional precautions to be incorporated into the design to reduce the risk to an acceptable level and if such reduction were not possible the proposal would be rejected. 3) The operator will be concerned to ensure that during the lifetime of the plant no changes take place in plant, staff or operating rules that will cause it to fall below the requirements implied by the criteria for acceptability.

The practical efficacy of the proposed risk acceptability Ranking Technique was tested against three potential major hazard cases: Canvey Island, Moss Morran and Rijnmond. These cases had in the past generated a certain amount of controversy so consequently there was a fairly comprehensive range of data available about them. The tests showed that Ranking the acceptability of these cases simply on the basis of the associated technical risk factors gave acceptability Ranking that was very similar to the overall Ranking of acceptability they had been given earlier. Further tests of the Technique were made by applying it to Channel Tunnel proposals and future energy supply options, these tests showed the more general capability of the Technique. An important conclusion from the tests was that the Ranking steps proposed were found to be practical, recognizable and broad enough to be detectable with the methods of calculation and data that have to be used in such cases. The tests also appear to justify the view that the proposed criteria are simple to apply in practice and that the transparency of the Technique has advantages, particularly in relation to presenting decisions about complex projects to the lay public. The simplicity of the presentation in no way undermines the quality of information needed to justify such decisions.

The possibility of practical alternatives to the proposed Ranking criteria was explored. From this exploration one conclusion reached was that there could be no qualitative alternative, as justification of Ranks simply in qualitative terms could be interpreted as expressing a lack of scientific and technical understanding of the characteristics of the activity being considered. However, for the preliminary stages of the assessment of a novel proposal, carefully structured analysis of the qualitative evidence can be helpful in identifying the optimum procedure to be followed to develop the quantitative evidence required to determine the acceptability of risks.

Although there are several ways a description of risk can be built up in quantitative terms there appears to be no way as satisfactory as using the proposed Ranking Technique. It is considered, that the criteria identified expressed in easily understandable, honest and comparable terms the way the information available could be assessed. Other ways of defining the criteria are either emotive or date or make comparison between countries difficult. There is no reason why the criteria proposed should not be used for assessing the acceptability of a wider range of complex proposals than just the risks specifically in the cases considered in this study. It is appreciated that for some forms of risk different criteria might be required, but the same general pattern of Ranking retained. Some general guidance was given on the use that can be made of the Ranking Technique in its present state of development by people with the appropriate skill. This guidance was particularly directed at the improvements in assessing risk acceptability identified by Layfield.

It is appreciated that the Ranking Technique can be iteratively refined to take account of experience gained with its use and new understandings that develop of the needs of decision making.

REFERENCES

1) CHICKEN J.C. and HAYNS M.R. A multi-factor criterion for risk
    acceptability, a paper presented at the 1984 annual meeting of
    the Society for Risk Analysis in Knoxville USA.
2) CHICKEN J.C. and HAYNS M.R. Development of the non-dimensional
    method of ranking risks, a paper presented at the 1985 annual
    meeting of the society for Risk Analysis in
    Washington USA.
3) KOUTSOYIANNIS A. Non-Price Decisions, Macmillan Press Ltd., 1982,
    London.
4) MILES M.B. and HUBERMAN A.M. Qualitative Data Analysis, Sage
    Publications, Beverly Hills, 1984.
5) CHAPMAN M. Decision Analysis, Civil Service College Handbook,
    HMSO, 1981, London.
6) PESTON M., CODDINGTON A. Statistical Decision Theory, Civil
    Service College Occasional Papers, HMSO, 1978, London.
7) HILTON G. Intermediate Politometrics, Columbia University Press,
    New York, 1982.
8) PEARCE D., EDWARDS L., BEURET G. Decision Making for Energy
    Futures, Macmillan Press Ltd. 1979, London.
9) CHICKEN J.C. Nuclear Power Hazard Control Policy, Pergamon
    Press, Oxford, 1982, pp 212-225.
10) VESELY W.E. and DAVIS T.C. Two Measures of Risk Importance and
    their Application, Nuclear Technology, Vol. 68, February 1985, pp
    226-234.
11) Definitely no can mean maybe, The Economist, 30th March 1985, pp
    91-92.
12) Thinking Machines, The Economist, 11th May 1985, pp 82-83.
13) HAYNS M.R. and UNWIN S.D. A method to incorporate uncertainty
    and degree of compliance in safety goals, a paper presented at
    the San Francisco Conference 1986.
14) CHICKEN J.C. Risk Assessment for Hazardous Installations,
    Pergamon Press, Oxford, 1986.
15) VINCK W.F., GILBY E.V., CHICKEN J.C. Quantified Safety
    Objectives in High Technology meaning and demonstration, a paper
    presented at the International ANS/ENS Topical meeting on Thermal
    Reactor Safety, San Diego, 2-6 Februry 1984.
16) VERSTEEG M.F. Risk-management as an administrative tool, for the
    Dutch government in their external safety policy. An integrated
    approach to nuclear and non-nuclear stationary potential sources.
    Directorate-General for the Environment Ministry of Housing,
    Physical Planning and Environment, The Netherlands.
17) 'NRC adopts policy statement on safety goalds for the operation
    of nuclear power plants' Nuclear Safety Vol. 27, No. 4, pp 555-
    556.
18) ANTHONY R.D. Safety and Licensing: the British Perspective,
    Nuclear Energy, Journal of the British Nuclear Energy Society,
    Vol. 25, No. 1, February 1986.
19) LAYFIELD SIR FRANK Report on the Sizewell 'B' Public Inquiry,
    Vol. 2, published by Her Majesty's Stationery Office, London,
    1987, R12 p 9.
20) MacGREGOR D. and SLOVIC P. Perceived acceptability of Risk
    Analysis, Vol. 6, No. 2, pp 245-256.

21)   HOLLAENDER A. Acceptance of the Distinguished Contribution Award of the Society for Risk Analysis, Risk Analysis, Vol. 6, No. 2, June 1986, p 114.
22)   COX D.C. and BAYBUTT P. Limit Lines for Risk, Nuclear Technology, Vol. 57, June 1982, pp 320-330.
23)   LAYFIELD SIR FRANK Report on the Sizewell 'B' Public Inquiry, Summary of Conclusions and Recommendations, published by Her Majesty's Stationery Office, London, 1987, C47, pp 20-23.
24)   Cmd 9389 a programme of Nuclear Power, Her Majesty's Stationery Office, London, February 1955, p 7.
25)   CHICKEN J.C. Risk Assessment for Hazardous Installations, Op.Cit., p 93-94.
26)   JONES-LEE M.W. The Political Economy of Physical Risk, a paper presented at the First International Conference on Risk Assessment of Chemicals and Nuclear Materials, Surrey University, September 1986.
27)   CHICKEN J.C. Nuclear Power Hazard Control Policy, Op.Cit., p 30.
28)   WILSON R. and CROUCH E.A.C. Risk/Benefit Analysis, Ballinger Publishing Co., Cambridge, Massachusetts, 1982, pp 77-78.
29)   LAYFIELD SIR FRANK Report on the Sizewell 'B' Public Inquiry Vol. 5, Chapter 54, pp 6-8, published by Her Majesty's Stationery Office, London, 1987.
30)   LAYFIELD SIR FRANK Report on the Sizewell 'B' Public Inquiry, Summary of Conclusions and Recommendations, published by Her Majesty's Stationery Office, London, 1987, C.47 p 11.
31)   MAY W.W. $'s for Lives: Ethical Considerations in the Use of Cost/Benefit Analysis by For-Profit Firms: Risk Analysis, Vol. 2, No. 1, March 1982, pp 35-46.
32)   SOLOMON K.A., WIPPLE C., OKRENT D. More on Insurance and Catastrophic Events: Can we Expect de facto Limits on Liability Recoveries? A paper presented at the ANS topical meeting Probablistic Analysis of Nuclear Reactor Safety, May 1978.
33)   PETTY SIR W. Political Arithmetic, or a Discourse Concerning the Extent and Value of Lands, People and Buildings, etc., London, Robert Clavell, 1699.
34)   SINCLAIR C., MARSTRAND P., NEWICK P. Innovations and human risk, published by the Centre for the Study of Industrial Innovation, London 1972, p 21.
35)   HICKS A.J. The Role of Insurance Safety, a paper presented to the OYEZ 1982 Review Seminar on Risk Management and Acceptability, April 1982, London.
36)   Accident Costing, published by the Risk Management Unit of Reed Stenhouse U.K. Ltd.,
37)   Insurance Facts and Figures 1981, British Insurance Association, London, p 201.
38)   BAMBER L. Safety Risks Will Cost You Money, The Engineer Survey, 26 April 1979, p 47.
39)   Daily Telegraph, 22nd March 1983, p 6.
40)   GRAHAM J.D. and VAUPEL J.W. Value of a Life: What Differences Does It Make? Risk Analysis, Vol. 1, No. 1, New York, March 1981, pp 89-95.
41)   HALL P. Great Planning Disasters, Penguin Books, 1980, p7.
42)   HANSARD, House of Commons Official Report, Vol. 88, No. 24, 9th December 1985, col. 707. Her Majesty's Stationery Office, London.

43) LAYFIELD SIR FRANK Sizewell 'B' Public Inquiry, Summary of Conclusions and Recommendations, Op.Cit. C2, pp 28-29.
44) BROWN J., LEE T. and FIELDING J. Concerns Worry and Anxiety about Hazard with Special Reference to Nuclear Power - a Secondary Analysis of Data Collected by Social Community Planning Research for the Health and Safety Executive, a report issued by the Psychology Department of the University of Surrey.
45) THOMAS K., MAURR D., FISHBEIN M., OTWAY H.J., HINKLE R.A, SIMPSON D., Comparative Study of Public Beliefs about Five Energy Systems. Paper RR-80-15, April 1980 published by the International Institute for Applied Systems Analysis, Laxenburg, Austria.
46) Nuclear Power Public Opinion, published by the Nuclear Energy Agency, OECD Paris, 1984, pp 66-72.
47) Nuclear Power and Public Opinion, Op.Cit. pp 73-79.
48) STALLEN P.J.M. and TOMAS A. Public Concern about Industrial Hazards, a paper presented at the annual meeting of the Society for Risk Analysis, Washington, USA, October 1985.
49) Public Opinion in the European Community on Energy in 1984, XVII/282/85-EN, a report published by the Commission of the European Communities Directorate-General for Energy.
50) Canvey· an investigation of potential hazards from operations in the Canvey Island/Thurrock area. A report by the Health and Safety Executive, published by Her Majesty's Stationery Office, London 1978.
51) Canvey: a second report, a review of potential hazards from operatons in the Canvey Island/Thurrock area three years after publication of the Canvey Report, published by Her Majesty's Stationery Office, London 1981, pp 14-15.
52) KUNREUTHER H.C., LINNEROTH J. Risk Analysis and Decision Processes, published by Springer Verlag, Berlin, 1983, pp 105-108.
53) Health and Safety Executive Report of the Steering Committee on radiofrequency ignition hazards at St. Fergus, Scotland, Her Majesty's Stationery Office London, February 1979.
54) Health and Safety Executive Report, 'A reappraisal of the HSE safety evluation of the proposed St. Fergus to Moss Morran LNG pipcline, Her Majesty's Stationery Office, London, September 1980.
55) KUNREUTHER H.C., LINNEROTH J. et al, Risk Analysis and Decision Processes, Op.Cit., pp 89-90.
56) The Race to Cross the Channel, The Illustrated London News, Volume 273, Number 7048, November 1985, pp 29-34.
57) Cmnd 8561 Fixed Channel Link Report of UK/French Study Group, Her Majesty's Stationery Office, London, June 1982.
58) Ridley ignores calls for Channel Inquiry, New Civil Engineer, 7th November 1985, p 9.
59) KUNREUTHER H.C., LINNEROTH J. et al, Risk Analysis and Decision Processes, Op.Cit., pp 154-177.
60) KUNREUTHER H.C., LINNEROTH J. et al, Risk Analysis and Decision Processes, Op.Cit., pp 113-122.
61) KUNREUTHER H.C., LINNEROTH J. et al, Risk Analysis and Decision Processes, Op.Cit. pp 64-80.
62) KUNREUTHER H.C., LINNEROTH J. et al, Risk Analysis and Decision Processes, Op.Cit., pp 76-86.

63) KUNREUTHER H.C., LINNEROTH J. et al, Risk Analysis and Decision Processes, Op.Cit., p 93.
64) Channel Fixed Link Environmental Appraisal of Alternative Proposal, Her Majesty's Stationery Office, London, December 1985.
65) HANSARD, House of Commons Official Report, Vol. 88, No. 24, 9th December 1985, Col. 707, Her Majesty's Stationery Office London.
66) HANSARD, House of Commons Report, Vol. 88 No. 24, Op.Cit., Cols 655-688.
67) Atom, No 356, June 1986, published by the United Kingdom Atomic Energy Authority, p 41.
68) Advances in Power Station Construction, produced by the Central Electricity Generating Board, published by Pergamon Press, Oxford, 1986, p 7.
69) Advances in Power Station construction, Op.Cit., pp 548-556.
70) Advances in Power Station construction, Op.Cit., p 333.
71) Tidal Power from the Severn Estuary, Volume 1, published by Her majesty's Stationery Office, London.
72) EUR 6417 Nuclear and Non-Nuclear Risk - An Exercise in Comparability, published by the Commission of the European Communities 1980, p 206.
73) EUR 6417, Op.Cit., p 206.
74) Cancer Risk from Coal, Nuclear Energy, Volume 23, No. 4, August 1984, published by the British Nuclear Energy Society, p 197.
75) LORD MARSHALL Nuclear Waste and Nimby, Atom, No. 356, June 1986, published by the United Kingdom Atomic Energy Authority pp 2-16.
76) BALDEWICZ et al, Historical Perspectives on Risk for Large-Scale Technological Systems, University of California, November 1974, p 93.
77) R no 2E. Guide for the classification of Hazardous Areas in Zones in Relation to Gas Explosion Hazard and to the Installation and Selection of Electrical Apparatus. Report of the Directorate-General of Labour. First Edition 1980, published by the Directorate-General of Labour at the Ministry of Social Affairs, Voorburg, The Netherlands, p 15.
78) Circular 984, Planning Controls over Hazardous Development, issued by the Department of the Environment and Welsh Office, March 1984, published by Her Majesty's Sationery Office, London.
79) LAYFIELD SIR FRANK Sizewell 'B' Public Inquiry, Op.Cit. paragraph 2.98.
80) LAYFIELD SIR FRANK Sizewell 'B' Public Inquiry, Op.Cit. paragraphs 2.127 to 2.134.
81) LAYFIELD SIR FRANK Sizewell 'B' Public Inquiry, Op.Cit., paragraphs 2.101 and 2.102.
82) Joint Airworthiness Requirements, JAW-AWO All Weather Operations, published by the Civil Aviation Authority, Cheltenham, July 1985, ACJ AWO 231.
83) VOGEL R.C. and WALL I.B. Some Observations on NUREG-1150, a paper presented at the Probabilistic Safety Assessment and Risk Management Conference PSA 87 held in Zurich September 1987.
84) MOSLEH A. et al, The elicitation and use of expert opinion in risk assessment: a critical review. A paper presented at the Probabilistic Safety Assessment and Risk Management Conference PSA 87 held in Zurich September 1987.

85) UNWIN S.D. A Fuzzy Set Theoretic Foundation for Use Uncertainty Analysis, Risk Analysis Vol. 6, No. 1, 1986, published by the Plenum Publishing Corporation, New York.
86) BUCKLEY J.J. Stochastic Cominance: An Approach to Decision Making under Risk. Risk Analysis Vol. 6, No. 1, 1986, published by Plenum Publishing Corporation, New York.

APPENDIX 1

SUMMARY OF THE ESSENTIAL FEATURES OF
THE RISK RANKING TECHNIQUE

The incentive for developing the Risk Ranking Technique was to provide decision makers involved, whether at the regulatory level or at the management level of a project, with a comprehensive assessment of the acceptability of the project.

Essentially the Technique consists of making an assessment of all the factors associated with the acceptability of the risks inherent in a project. For analytical purposes the factors are considered under the three broad headings of:- technical, economic and socio-political. These three groups of factors are intended to cover every aspect of acceptability and taken together they provide a realistic basis for Ranking the overall acceptability of a proposal. The acceptability of each group of factors being scored on a scale 0 to 4. The higher the score the lower the factor's acceptability. The overall Ranking of the acceptability of a project being calculated by integrating the scores of the individual factors. Table 1.1 shows how the definition of risk Rank is constructed.

TABLE 1.1   CONSTRUCTION OF RISK RANK

RISK RANK	ACCEPTABILITY	POSSIBLE ACTION TO MAKE RANKING MORE ACCEPTABLE	INDIVIDUAL FACTOR SCORE RANGE	TOTAL SCORE RANGE
1	Unlikely	Unlikely any possible	No factor greater than 4	>6-12
2	Only if risk can be reduced	Organizational and technical	No factor greater than 3	>4-6
3	Subject to certain action	Organizational	No factor greater than 2	>3-4
4	Without restriction	None required	No factor greater than 1	>0-2

Ranks 2 and 3 are both Rankings of proposals that can be made universally acceptable by modifying the proposal. The changes required to make a Rank 2 proposal acceptable being much more extensive than required to make a Rank 3 proposal acceptable.

To some extent the success of the Ranking Technique depends on having available a relevant reliable analysis of the conditions of interest.

It is important that the significance of any errors built into the analysis is established. But the Technique is also useful when, as is often the case in decision making, there is little or no data available, as in such cases the Technique provides a logical structure to the analysis.

To make proper use of the Technique some quantitative relationship has to be established between acceptability Rank score and the quantitative characteristics of the factors. Ranking acceptability of technical factors has been related, as shown in Table 1.2 to the risk of death per year. Table 1.2 is essentially a criteria for scoring the acceptability of technical factors for Ranking. In a similar way criteria for Ranking scoring and economic and socio-political factors can be developed. One form these relationships can take for economic and socio-political Ranking critieria is shown in Tables 1.3 and 1.4. It is stressed that the criteria adopted have to be tailored to suit the specific decision making environment involved. At the same time it is important the criteria are kept the same within a particular family of uses of the Technique otherwise the advantage of consistency of the Technique will be compromised. A simplified flow sheet for applying the Ranking Technique is given in Fig. 1.1.

TABLE 1.2   DEFINITION OF CRITERIA THAT HAVE BEEN USED FOR SCORING TECHNICAL ACCEPTABILITY

ACCEPTABILITY	ASHBY CRITERIA RISK OF DEATH PER YEAR	SCORE RANGE	EQUIVALENT RISK ACCEPTABLE RANK
Unlikely to be acceptable	one in 1,000	3 - 4	1
Only acceptable if risk can be reduced	one in 10,000	2 - 3	2
Yes, subject to detailed adjustments to the proposal being made	one in 100,000	1 - 2	3
Yes, without restriction	one in 1,000,000	0 - 1	4

In the normal course of events there will be a band of uncertainty associated with the data that has to be used for Ranking. The decision maker will want to explore the significance of the uncertainty. To satisfy this need Rankings can be made based on data representing both the upper and lower levels of uncertainty. This will give the decision maker a deeper understanding of the confidence that can be placed in the Ranking. A description of the uncertainty of the Ranking Technique is shown diagrammatically in Fig. 1.2. In Chapter 10 of the main text, there is more detailed discussion about

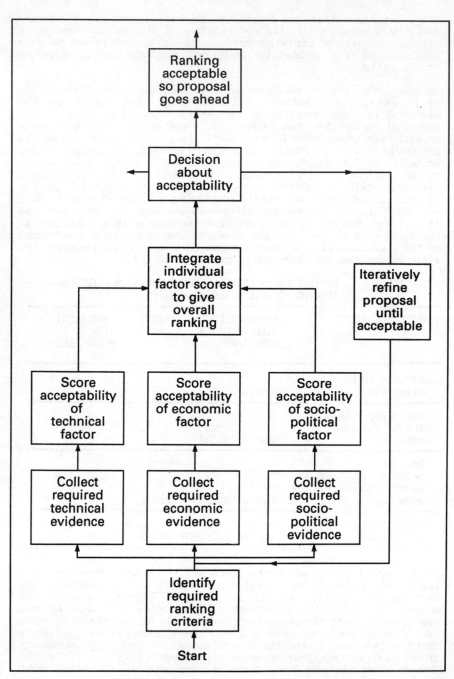

Fig 1.1 Flowsheet for application of ranking technique

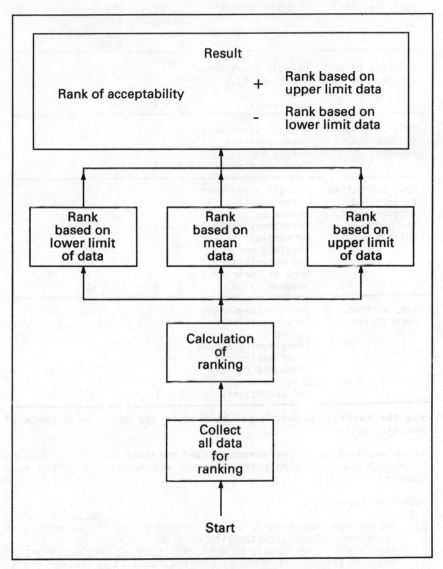

Fig 1.2 Ranking description of uncertainty

TABLE 1.3   POSSIBLE RELATIONSHIP BETWEEN ECONOMIC FACTORS
AND THE RANKING SCORE

ACCEPTABILITY	ECONOMIC FACTORS	SCORE RANGE	EQUIVALENT RISK ACCEPTABILITY RANK
Unlikely to be acceptable	Overall assessment shows negative return on investment	3 - 4	1
Only acceptable if risk can be reduced	Overall assessment shows positive return on investment doubtful	2 - 3	2
Yes, subject to to detailed adjustments to the proposal being made	Overall assessment shows positive return on investment could be marginal if all possible errors and uncertainty were at their most adverse value	1 - 2	3
Yes, without restriction	Overall assessment shows positive return on investment adequate after making due allowance for all possible erros and uncertainty	0 - 1	4

how the Ranking Technique can be used to explore a wide range of
decision options.

In an examination of the advantages and disadvantages of the Ranking
Technique the following points for and against the technique were
found[1]:-

Points in favour:-

1)   The method introduces a logical structure into the comprehensive
     assessment of the acceptability of risk.
2)   The method is applicable to most risk acceptability questions.
3)   The non-dimensional form of Ranking means the findings can be
     presented in an unemotive way that make them easier for the
     general public to assimilate.
4)   The result can be refined as better data becomes available.
5)   If used for regulatory purposes the Ranks would give the proposer
     an easier target to aim at.

TABLE 1.4   POSSIBLE RELATIONSHIP BETWEEN SOCIO-POLITICAL
FACTORS AND THE RANKING SCORE

ACCEPTABILITY	SOCIO-POLITICAL FACTORS	SCORE RANGE	EQUIVALENT RISK ACCEPTABILITY RANK
Unlikely to be acceptable	Less than 1/3rd of the population judged to be in favour of the proposal	3 - 4	1
Only acceptable if risk can be reduced	Between 1/3rd and 1/2 of the relevant population judged to be in favour of the proposal	2 - 3	2
Yes, subject to detailed adjustments to the proposal being made	Between 1/2 and 2/3rds of the population judged to be in favour of the proposal	1 - 2	3
Yes without restriction	Over 2/3rds of population judged to be in favour of the proposal	0 - 1	4

Points against:-

1)   The comprehensive nature of the Ranking Technique complicates the
     decision making process.
2)   The Technique could be regarded as a way of hiding unpalatable
     facts.
3)   If adopted as criteria proposals have to satisfy Ranking could be
     regarded as removing a degree of freedom from the regulatory
     authorities.

Reference:-

1)   CHICKEN J.C. Comprehensive Assessment. A paper presented at the
     First International Conference on Risk Assessment of Chemicals
     and Nuclear Materials, held at the University of Surrey,
     September 1986.

APPENDIX 2

DEFINITIONS

BEAUFORT SCALE
Divides wind conditions into thirteen grades, from 0 which is calm with wind speeds less than 0.2 metres/sec to wind speed 12 when the wind is faster than 32.7 metres/sec

COMPREHENSIVE DECISIONS
Decisions involving consideration of technical, economic and socio-political factors.

CSX VALUE
Cost of saving one extra statistical life.

DECISION HEIGHT
Which height above runway by which go-around must be initiated unless a safe landing can be made.

DELPHI TECHNIQUE
Finding a consensus view by iterative consultation with a panel of experts.

DIRECT RISK
Damage and injury on a site involved.

EXPERT
Independent advisor.

EXPLAINED VARIABLE
The dependent variable, or the single term in an equation that explained by the several other terms in the equation.

EXPLANATORY VARIABLE
The independent variable or terms in an equation that expain the explained variable.

FLARE
Change to commitment to landing from cruising conditions.

FUZZY DATA
Data that is not clearly defined.

FUZZY SET
A set of elements whose limits are not clearly defined.

GNP
Gross National Product, the total value of all goods and services produced in a country in a year.

GO-AROUND
Transition from an approach to a stabilised climb.

HARD DATA
Perfect defect free quantitative data directly relevant to the proposition being assessed.

ILS
Instrument Landing System.

INDIRECT RISK — Consequential losses like loss of production, harm to people outside the site and loss of customers.

MACRO ECONOMIC — Economic factors large enough to influence national or international economics.

NET EFFECTIVE COST (NEC) — Net cost of supplying electricity from a new power station, expressed in terms of an annual charge per KW averaged over the life of a power station. It is derived from an estimate of the cost of building and operating the station less any benefits from savings in operating costs elsewhere in the power system. An NEC which is negative shows that the additional costs of the new power station are outweighed by cost savings elsewhere in the system, and that the new station would be cost saving over its lifetime.

OBJECTIVE DATA — Based on observation or measurement.

OBJECTIVE VIEW — Based on quantitative scientific evidence.

OPPORTUNITY COST — Cost of foregone alternatives. This is a way of showing that, as resources are always limited, having more of one thing means having less of something else.

PAYOFF — The final result in units appropriate to the decision being analysed, these any may be probability on event, money or some measure of acceptability.

PROBABILITY RISK ASSESSMENT (PRA) — A particular application of PSA where the risk posed by the plant is explicitly evaluated.

PROBABILISTIC SAFETY ASSESSMENT (PSA) — The combination of calculational methods for plant reliability and the consequences of plant failures to provide an overall methodology for evaluating plant safety.

PROPOSER — Proposer or body sponsoring a project.

QUALITATIVE DATA — Data based on opinion expressed in non-quatitative terms.

QUANTITATIVE DATA — Data based on measurement specifies the characteristics or behaviour of material or a component numerically.

RICHTER SCALE   Divides the magnitude of earthquakes into eleven Ranks according to the amount of energy released. Rank 0 is equal to the explosion of 175mg of TNT or a man jumping from a table. Rank 10 is equal to the explosion of 7,000 megatons of TNT or 350 hydrogen bombs.

RISK   The probability of an undesired outcome. In relation to economic arguments it can mean the undesired outcome expressed in monetary terms.

SIMPLE DECISIONS   Decisions involving considerations of only one group of factors, which may be technical, economic or socio-political.

SOFT DATA   Qualitative data of doubtful validity or relevance.

SUBJECTIVE DATA   Based on opinion.

SUBJECTIVE VIEW   Non-specialist views, such as public opinion.

TOTAL RISK   The sum of direct and indirect risks.

TRUE POINTS   A data point that belongs to the set of data being considered.

UNCERTAINTY   The magnitude of doubt in either qualitative or quantitative terms.

UNCERTAIN DATA   Data about which there is no indication of the associated probability distribution.

UNCERTAIN PARAMETER   Parameter about which there is no or very little knowledge.

UTILITY   An analyst's measure of a proposal's benefit compared to the benefit that would result from spending the money involved in different ways.

WILD POINT   A false data point that can be confidently neglected.

APPENDIX 3

RANGE OF TECHNICAL ACCEPTABILITY CRITERIA

Specification of technical acceptability is generally discussed either in terms of point values or range values. A point value does not give an adequate description of the parameters associated with defining acceptability of complex projects, which by their very nature have a range of risk values associated with them. A point value can perhaps be used to define a firm limit when there is an implied relation between the point value and the range of values. With both point and range values there is concern about errors and uncertainty in the data and calculatons that have to be used to justify that the criteria have been satisfied.

Although this study is concerned with decisions about acceptability in general it is helpful to look at the approach to technical risk acceptability that has been adopted by the aircraft industry as it represents good practice. The airworthiness requirements adopted by most countries are generally those drawn up by the Airworthiness Authorities Steering Committee and referred to as the Joint Airworthiness Requirements. It is not without interest that these requirements have been accepted by the countries that have signed the "Arrangements Concerning the Development and the Acceptance of Joint Airworthiness Requirements". In these requirements it is recognized that during flight testing to prove compliance with requirements some tolerance on the various factors must be allowed for. Examples of how tolerances are written into the measured requirements are: the way it is specified during flight testing that aircraft weight can vary by +5%, -10%, airspeed can vary by plus or minus 3 knots or 3% which ever is higher and power can vary by plus or minus 5%.[1] These tolerances have to be taken into account in determining the take-off decision speed and other critical speeds.[2]

For all weather operation with an automatic pilot the probability limits recognized include the following[3]:

Longitudinal touch down earlier than a point on the runway 60m from the threshold average 10^{-6} and limit 10^{-5}.
Bank angle such that the wing tip touches the ground before the wheels average 10^{-8} and limit 10^{-7}.

The limit value is the probability of occurence if one variable is held at its most adverse value, while the other variables vary according to their probability distributions.

In demonstrating compliance of an aircraft with the requirement that not more than 5% of automated approaches should terminate in a go-around below 150m, a whole series of criteria must be satisfied. These criteria include the requirement that 95% of approaches from 150m are completed without a systems failure. Fig. 3.1 which is reproduced from the Joint Airworthiness Requirements* relates

---

* Reproduced with permission of the CAA

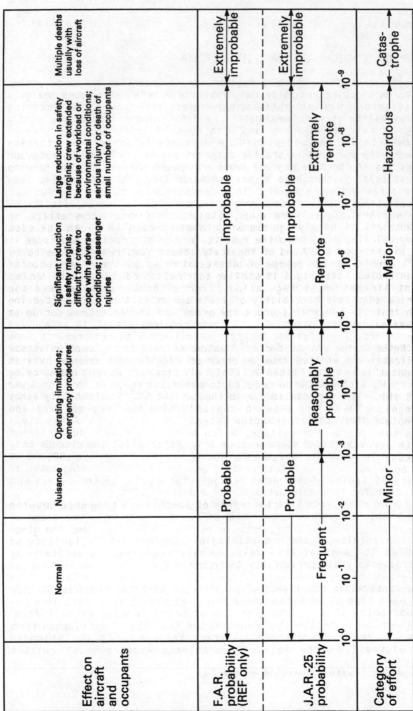

Fig 3.1 Quantitative and qualitative statement of Joint Airworthiness Requirement for acceptability

quantitative statements about acceptability to qualitative descriptions of accuracy.

This simple outline of the practices employed by the aircraft industry shows how the authorities recognize the statistical distribution associated with the various factors they have to assess to determine airworthiness acceptability. The other important point about the very detailed Joint Airworthiness Requirements is that they are accepted and worked to internationally.

In relation to the acceptability of the risks associated with any potentially hazardous installations, the significance of the range of risks and the uncertainty and errors in predicting risks also have to be assessed. Although to a certain extent these factors overlap they do not replace each other. In a demonstration of how the Nuclear Installations Inspectorate's principles could be satisfied, studies of two national cases were made, these studies show the effect of uncertainty.[5] On average the uncertainty associated with the case study calculations caused the results to span an order of magnitude at the lower probability end of the scale, that is at probabilities below 10^{-6}. Expressing the range of uncertainty that has to be allowed for as an order of magnitude is similar to the difference allowed, by the Joint Airworthiness Regulations, for the difference between the average and limit probability of the bank angle of an aircraft being such that the wing tip touches the ground before the wheels during an automated landing.

The Netherlands Risk Criteria,[6] which is intended to be of universal application shows more than an order of magnitude difference between acceptable and unacceptable. This allowance is identified as being for risks that should be reduced to make them acceptable. In some ways this allowance is similar to the two steps in acceptability Ashby recognized as being between the unlikely to be acceptable and acceptable without reservation categories.[7] The two Ashby steps span two orders of magnitude, which are: if the individual risk of death per year is of the order of 1 in 10,000 then the risk is only acceptable if it can be reduced, and if the risk is one in 100,000 it can be acceptable subject to certain engineering action being taken to reduce it.

From this it seems that two orders of magnitude difference between acceptable and unacceptable risks are widely accepted. One order of magnitude being for uncertainty in estimating the risk and the other order of magnitude being for uncertainty about the acceptability of the risk in general. Also there are finite upper and lower limits to the range of risks. The upper limit being the risk of an individual being killed should not exceed 1 in 1,000 per year and the lower limit being 1 in 1,000,000 of an individual being killed or 1 in 100,000,000 of several hundred or more being killed.

Although the definitions of technical acceptability just described are drawn from specific industries the concept of defining technical acceptability in quantitative terms is applicable to most projects with a technical content.

The definitions of the range and limits of technical risk acceptability described appear to endorse the way the steps have been specified in the Ranking Technique. The quantitative specification of acceptability implies, somewhat optimistically that there are crisp quantitiative data derived from some kind of real life experience on which to base the assessment of acceptability. However, it has to be recognized that for various reasons decisions sometimes have to be based on expert opinion. If decisions have to be based on qualitative opinion then great care is needed in its collection and assessment to determine the confidence that can be put in it.

CONCLUSIONS

The following conclusions appear to be justified:-

1) The Joint Airworthiness Requirements show how there can be international agreement about the way technical requirements can be specified in detail in quantitative terms. This is an example that could be followed generally for determining acceptable reliability of performance.
2) Any definition of acceptability has to allow for uncertainty in calculations and measurements justifying acceptability.
3) Particular care is needed in establishing the confidence that can be placed in qualitative data based in expert opinion views based on such opinion must be tested.

REFERENCES

1) JAR-25 Joint Airworthiness Requirements, Large Aeroplanes, published by the Civil Aviation Authority, Cheltenham, revised up to 17.3.86, section JAR 25.21.d.
2) JAR-25 Joint Airworthiness Requirements, Op.Cit., section JAR 25.107.
3) JAR-AWO Joint Airworthiness Requirements, All Weather Operations, published by the Civil Aviation Authority, Cheltenham, amended up to 29.11.85, section ACJ AWO 131.1.4.
4) JAR-AWO Joint Airworthiness Requirements, All Weather Operations, Op.Cit., section ACJ, AWO 231.1.
5) VINCK W.F., GILBY E.V., and CHICKEN J.C. Quantified Safety Objectives in High Technology; Meaning and Demonstration, a paper presented at the International ANS/ENS Topical Meeting on Thermal Reactor Safety, held in San Diego, USA, February 1986.
6) VERSTEEG M.F. Risk-management as an administrative tool for the Dutch government in their external safety policy. An integrated approach to nuclear and non-nuclear stationary potential hazardous sources. Ministry of Housing, Physical Planning and Environment, Directorate-General for the Environment, Leidschendom, The Netherlands.
7) ASHBY LORD Reconciling Man with the Environment, Oxford University Press, 1978.

APPENDIX 4

A SUMMARY OF THE POLICY STATEMENT OF US NUCLEAR REGULATORY
COMMISSION ON SAFETY GOALS

	QUALITATIVE SAFETY GOALS	QUANTITATIVE SAFETY GOALS
Individual Risk	Individual members of the public should be provided with a level of protection from the consequences of nuclear power plant operations such that individuals bear no significant risk to life and health.	The risk to an average individual in the vicinity of a nuclear power plant of prompt fatalities that might result from reactor accidents should not exceed one tenth of one percent of the sum of prompt fatality risks resulting from other accidents to which members of the US population are generally exposed.
Social Risk	Societal risks to life and health from the operation of nuclear power plants should be comparable to or less than the risks of generating electricity by viable competing technologies and should not be a significant addition to other societal risk.	The risk to the population in the area of a nuclear power plant of cancer fatalities that might result from nuclear power plant operation should not exceed one tenth of one percent of the sum of cancer fatality risk resulting from all other causes.
Additional Rule	Severe core damage accidents can lead to more serious accidents with the potential for life-threatening off-site releases of radiation, for evacuation of members of the public and for contamination of public property. Apart from their health and safety consequences, such accidents can erode public confidence in the safety of nuclear power and can lead to further instability and unpredictability for the industry. In order to avoid these adverse consequences the Commission intends to pursue a regulatory program that has as its objective providing reasonable assurance, giving appropriate consideration to the uncertainties involved, that a severe core damage accident will not occur at a US nuclear power plant.	
General Guideline	Consistent with the traditional defense-in-depth approach and accident mitigation philosophy requiring reliable performance of containment systems, the overall mean frequency of a large release of radio-activity materials to the environment from a reactor accident should be less than one in one million per year of reactor operation.	

APPENDIX 5

STEPS IN REACTOR LICENSING PROCEDURE

The steps in licensing a reactor have similar characteristics to the steps involved in obtaining approval for any major novel potentially hazardous project. The approval of a new passenger aeroplane or a new drug are very similar. Regulatory authorities lay down the principles and they will judge acceptability by, then the proposer has to demonstrate how he will satisfy the principles.

The following are the six main steps that the Central Electricity Generating Board (CEGB) expect a reactor proposal to go through in order to obtain a license to operate at full power.[1]

1) The Generating Board lays down Design Safety Criteria designers are to use. The criteria cover: external hazards that have to be taken into account in the design, permissible radiation doses to the public and operators, permissible activity release, required integrity of components, engineered safeguards that must be incorporated and protective device requirements.
2) Prepare and submit to the Nuclear Installations Inspectorate (NII) a Preliminary Safety Report describing: essential features of the design, how the design will satisfy the CEGB's criteria, and how the design will satisfy the regulatory authorities principles, preliminary analysis of critical fault conditions, preliminary assessment of the proposed safeguards and details of the research and development programme to be undertaken to substantiate claims made.
3) When the Preliminary Safety Report is accepted by the licensing authority a Pre-Construction Safety Report will be produced, which will amplify and fill in the details of the claims made about the design in the Preliminary safety report. When the Pre-Construction Safety Report is accepted by the licensing authority they will issue a Site Licence which will allow the CEGB to proceed with construction subject to obtaining consent for each stage of construction.
4) During construction CEGB will keep the NII informed about the relevant results obtained from research and development work and any design problems with safety implications that arise.
5) Not less than six months before the date it is intended to start loading fuel an updated version of the Preliminary Safety Report will be submitted to NII. On the basis of this report NII will be asked to give their consent to allowing fuel loading to start.
6) When commissioning tests and fuel loading are complete a report will be prepared showing how the design intent and all requirements have been satisfied. This report will be submitted to NII with the request that they approve operation at power to start and the power level to be gradually increased to full power.

Ref.1: Advances in Power Station Construction produced by CEGB Barnwood, published by Pergamon Press Oxford, 1986, pp 75-76.

BIBLIOGRAPHY

ANTHONY R.D. Safety and Licensing: the British Perspective, Nuclear Energy, Journal of the British Nuclear Energy Society, Vol. 25, No. 1, February 1986.

ASHBY LORD Reconciling Man with the Environment, Oxford Unversity Press, 1978.

BAMBER L. Safety Risks Will Cost You Money, The Engineer Survey, 26 April 1979, p 47.

BALDEWICZ et al, Historial Perspectives on Risk for Large-Scale Technological Systems, University of California, November 1974, p 93.

BROWN J., LEE T. and FIELDING J. Concerns Worry and Anxiety about Hazard with Special Reference to Nuclear Power - a Secondary Analysis of Data Collected by Social Community Planning Research for the Health and Safety Executive, a report issued by the Psychology Department of the University of Surrey.

BUCKLEY J.J. Stochastic Cominance: An Approach to Decision Making Under Risk. Risk Analysis Vol. 6, No. 1, 1986, published by Plenum Publishing Corporation, New York.

CATTANEO F., DeSANCTIS S., GARRIBA S.F., VOLTA G. Learning from Abnormal Occurences: Results of a Fuzzy Analysis, A paper presented at the PSA '87 Conference, Zurich 1987.

CHAPMAN M. Decision Analysis, Civil Service College Handbook, HMSO, 1981, London.

CHICKEN J.C. Nuclear Power Hazard Control Policy, Pergamon Press, Oxford, 1982.

CHICKEN J.C. Risk Assessment for Hazardous Installations, Pergamon Press, Oxford, 1986.

CHICKEN J.C. Comprehensive Assessment. A paper presented at the First International Conference on Risk Assessment of Chemicals and Nuclear Materials, held at the University of Surrey, September 1986.

CHICKEN J.C. and HAYNS M.R. A multi-factor criterion for risk acceptability, a paper presented at the 1984 annual meeting of the Society for Risk Analysis in Knoxville USA.

CHICKEN J.C. and HAYNS M.R. Development of the non-dimensional method of ranking risks, a paper presented at the 1985 annual meeting of the Society for Risk Analysis in Washington USA.

COOK I., UNWIN S.D. NUREG/CR-4514 Controlling Principles for Prior Probability Assignments in Nuclear Risk Assessment, published by the U.S. Nuclear Regulatory Commission, 1986.

COX D.C. and BAYBUTT P. Limit Lines for Risk, Nuclear Technology, Vol. 57, June 1982, pp 320-330.

GRAHAM J.C. and VAUPEL J.W. Value of a Life: What Difference Does It Make? Risk Analysis, Vol. 1, No. 1, New York, March 1981, pp 89-95.

HALL P. Great Planning Disasters, Penguin Books, 1980.

HAYNS M.R. and UNWIN S.D. A method to incorporate uncertainty and degree of compliance in safety goals, a paper presented at the San Francisco Conference, 1986.

HICKS A.J. The Role of Insurance Safety, a paper presented to the OYEZ 1982 Review Seminar on Risk Management and Acceptability, April 1982, London.

HILTON G. Intermediate Politometrics, Columbia University Press, New York, 1982.

117

118

HOLLAENDER A. Acceptance of the Distinguished Contribution Award of the Society for Risk Analysis, Risk Analysis, Vol. 6, No. 2, June 1986, p 114.
HORSAK R.D. and DAMICO S.A. Risk Evaluation of Hazardous Waste Disposal Sites using Fuzzy Set Analysis published in Risk Assessment and Management edited by Love L.B., published by Plenum Press, New York, 1987, pp 643-648.
JONES-LEE M.W. The Political Economy of Physical Risk, a paper presented at the First International Conference on Risk Assessment of Chemicals and Nuclear Materials, Surrey University, September 1986.
KOUTSOYIANNIS A. Non-Price Decisions, Macmillan Press Ltd., 1982, London.
KUNREUTHER H.C., LINNEROTH J. Risk Analysis and Decision Processes, published by Springer Verlag, Berlin, 1983.
LAYFIELD SIR FRANK Report on the Sizewell 'B' Public Inquiry, published by Her Majesty's Stationery Office, London, 1987.
MacGREGOR D., SLOVIC P. Perceived Acceptability of Risk Analysis, Vol. 6, No. 2, pp 245-256.
MARSHALL LORD Nuclear Waste and Nimby, Atom, No. 356, June 1986, published by the United Kingdom Atomic Energy Authority.
MAY. W.W. $'s for Lives: Ethical Considerations in the Use of Cost/Benefit Analysis by For-Profit Firms: Risk Analysis, Vol. 2, No. 1, March 1982, pp 35-46.
MILES M.B. and HUBERMAN A.M. Qualitative Data Analysis, Sage Publications, Beverley Hills, 1984.
MOSLEH A. et al The elicitation and use of expert opinion in risk assessment: a critical review. A paper presented at the Probabilistic Safety Assessment and Risk Management Conference PSA '87 held in Zurch, September 1987.
PETTY SIR W. Political Arithmetic, or a Discourse Concerning the Extent and Value of Lands, People and Buildings, etc., London, Robert Clavell, 1699.
PRESTON M., CODDINGTON A. Statistical Decision Theory, Civil Service College College Occasional Papers, HMSO, 1978, London.
PREYSSL C. "Fuzzy Risk" Analysis Theory and Application published by International Institute for Applied System Analysis, Laxenburg Austria, 1986.
SINCLAIR C., MARSTRAND P., NEWICK P. Innovations and human risk, published by the Centre for the Study of Industrial Innovation, London 1972, p 21.
SOLOMON K.A., WIPPLE C., OKRENT D. More on Insurance and Catastrophic Events: Can we Expect de facto Limits on Liability Recoveries? A paper presented at the ANS topical meeting Probablistic Analysis of Nuclear Reactor Safety, May 1978.
STALLEN P.J.M. and THOMAS A. Public Concern about Industrial Hazards, a paper presented at the annual meeting of the Society for Risk Analysis, Washington, USE, October 1985.
THOMAS K., MAURR D., FISHBEIN M., OTWAY H.J., HINKLE R.A., SIMPSON D. Comparative Study of Public Beliefs about Five Energy Systems. Paper RR-80-15, April 1980 published by the International Institute for Applied Systems Analysis, Laxenburg Austria.
UNWIN S.D. A fuzzy set Theorectic Foundation for Use in Uncertainty Analysis, Risk Analysis Vol. 6, No. 1, 1986, published by the Plenum Publishing Corporation, New York.

VERSTEEG M.F. Risk-management as an administrative tool for the Dutch government in their external safety policy. An integrated approach to nuclear and non-nuclear stationary potential hazardous sources. Ministry of Housing, Physical Planning and Environment, Directorate-General for the Environment, Leidschendom, The Netherlands.

VINCK W.F., GILBY E.V. and CHICKEN J.C. Quantified Safety Objectives in High Technology; Meaning and Demonstration, a paper presented at the International ANS/ENS Topical Meeting on Thermal Reactor Safety, held in San Diego, USA, February 1986.

VOGEL R.C. and WALL I.B. Some Observations on NUREG-1150, a paper presented at the Probabilistic Safety Assessment and Risk Management Conference PSA '87 held in Zurich September 1987.

WILSON R. and CROUCH E.A.C. Risk/Benefit Analysis, Ballinger Publishing Co., Cambridge, Massachusetts, 1982.

Index

120

Index